Stories Jesus Told

Contents

Thanks to everyone who has made all of this possible, especially Lighthouse at Holy Trinity, Aylesbury, Alison Cotterall, and my husband David

Getting Started

Welcome to STORIES JESUS TOLD - a book of resource material, songs, stories, visual aids and activities to use in your toddler groups, pram services, family days and even (with a little bit of thought) family services.

All of this material is based on the idea of parents and children learning together. In this book we offer you 10 sessions all on the theme "Stories Jesus Told":

- The Great Feast
- The Mustard Seed
- The Lost Sheep
- The Lost Coin
- The Lost Son

- The Pharisee and the Tax Collector
- The Two Sons
- The Good Samaritan
- The Poor Widow's Gift
- The Houses on the Rock and the Sand

We have tried to start from a child's needs, emotions, interests, and from their world, which is centred around family and immediate neighbourhood. We hope that this material will help both parents and children to learn something of the joy of knowing Jesus.

Please note that, for each book, copying of templates and instructions is limited to their use with a group of up to ten children.

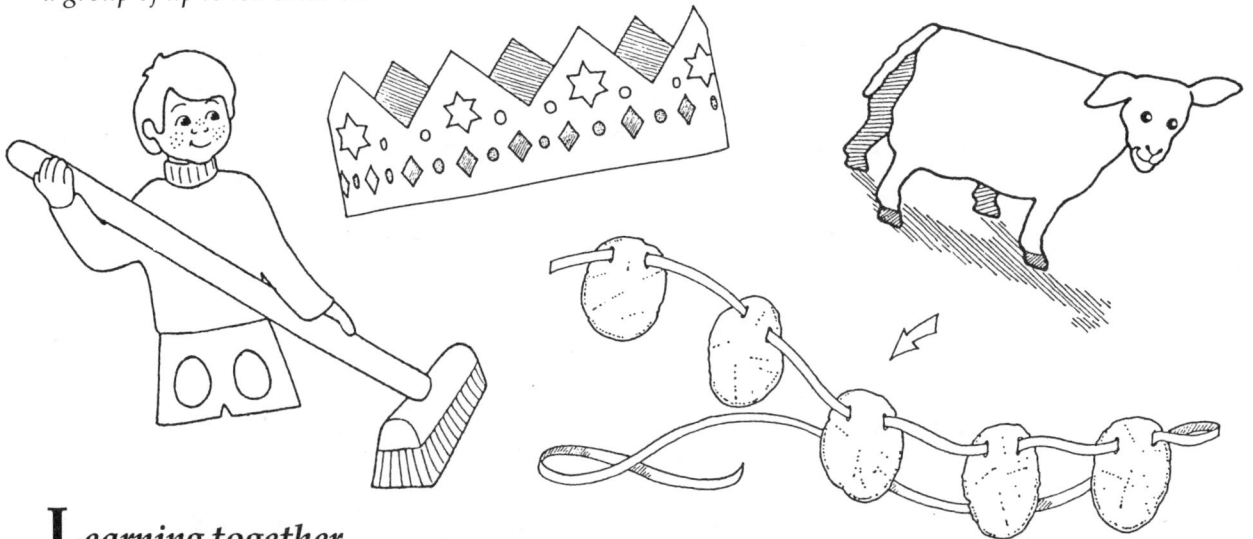

Learning together

All the ideas that follow are based on the aim of parents and children working together. They have been tried and tested with our own group, a place where parents could welcome their friends and neighbours, where church baptism links could be followed up, and where parents could be helped to keep the promises they made at their child's baptism.

If you are using this material to lead a group of your own, you might find the following helpful.

❶ Arrive early, preferably with helpers, to set up the room and activity. Welcome people as they arrive.

❷ *About 20-25 minutes:*
- Welcome
- Singing
- Story with big visual aid
- Prayer - to conclude the story
- Craft activity

❸ *About 30-35 minutes:*
- Free time together with coffee, orange juice and toys
- Tidy up toys
- Closing prayer

❹ Tidy the room and leave it as you found it.

A one-hour session should give plenty of time to talk together and get to know each other. You will have already broken the ice while doing the activity as everybody tried to stop their children glueing their fingers to whatever they were making!

Don't panic!
You might feel a bit intimidated by all of this, but don't be, it is all here to help. This material is yours now. Have fun, and adapt it for your situation. Enjoy learning together.

Having a party

Parties are fun (or they should be!). Children enjoy them. But why do we have parties?

Jesus seemed to spend a lot of his time enjoying himself with people, so much so that he was criticized for it! If our parent and under five groups are happy, joyful places then this should be reflected in the way we enjoy ourselves.

Here are some things that we have found useful in organizing parties for our groups.
- Work out a running order for the party.
- Have different members of the team responsible for different sections.
- Try to fit parties into your usual time and session; they don't need to be any longer.

Games

Pass the Parcel: with groups of over 10 children, have more than one parcel doing the rounds; don't use too much sellotape; use old Christmas or birthday wrapping paper rather than old newspaper.

For a group involving 0-3 year olds, 8 to 10 layers is plenty; use live music or a cassette, not a radio; pop music is often better than nursery rhymes because rhymes are very short and have too many gaps in between.

Games like "Simon Says" and Musical Statues are good because all the children can join in but they don't actually play with each other. Younger children are not very good at this. In this sort of game participation is the most important thing, so you don't need winners and no one needs to be eliminated.

Activity games like Ring a Ring a Roses, Here We Go Round the Mulberry Bush, and the Okey Cokey can be enjoyed by children from 18 months upwards.

It is useful to remember not to play any one game for too long.

Toys

If your group involves a large proportion of 0-3s, you might well want to have the toys out as a part of the party, not least because children this age can't cope with too many co-operating games. They are still very individual but enjoy playing in the company of others. It also gives the parents the chance to sit down and chat for a few minutes.

Singing

If your group usually sings, then it is a good idea to have a singing spot in the party. Singing is a good starter as it brings everyone together and it is easy for latecomers to join in. Singing can also quieten children down, so you might want to have it before the food is served.

Food

Remember that food at parties for under 5s usually will not be replacing a meal.

A suggested menu is:
- potato snacks, cheese snacks, and cheesy biscuits
- small cubes of cheese and sausages (forget the sticks)
- buns made in small *petit four* cases, with a basic sponge mix and a topping
- chocolate fingers and chocolate animals
- orange squash

And don't forget your parents: a slice of cake, mince pies, tea or coffee. Keep this food separate from the children's tea.

It is a good idea to have the children sitting at tables as this should reduce mess. Use either a paper plate or a serviette to act as a plate for each child.

Have all the children sitting down before you serve the drink. Try to avoid using thin paper or plastic throw-away cups. You could ask your parents to bring feeder beakers for the smaller children, and only fill them half full at the most.

Parents with children up to 18 months can sit with the children on their knee while other parents help from behind, or sit at the table.

Note. In the Unit for the Great Feast the party is only to give an idea of one, so don't go to town on it. A few savoury biscuits or crisps, a cake and a drink is all that is needed.

Money

Will the money from other sessions subsidize the party? Will parents pay subs as normal on the party day?

If it is a Christmas or end-of-term party, will you be giving a gift? Will the church give you any extra money to help finance this?

How to make a stick face puppet

You will need:
- some scrap paper
- A4 or A5 sized card
- small green garden sticks
- scissors
- parcel tape or strong sellotape
- medium/thick black marker pen

What to do:

❶ Using an area about 15cm x 21cm, practise drawing out your face design on to scrap paper. If you really can't draw then trace the face from a book. The Palm Tree Press, Butterworth and Inkpen books (see bibliography) have very good expressive faces for Bible stories, and they are easy to trace. Or you could use the "Help I Can't Draw" books available through CPAS.

❷ Once you have your design, copy out the outline onto your A4 or A5 piece of card and cut it out.

❸ Fill in face features, eyes, nose, mouth, beard, hair, etc. using marker pen.

❹ Stick the face on to the garden stick using the tape.

❺ Animal faces can be done in the same way.

❻ For groups of animals or people stick three or four faces on to backing card and attach them to the stick in the same way. You can make your puppets happy and sad, or sick and healthy by drawing the same face twice but with the different expressions and sticking them back to back with the stick in between them.

To make a card stand-up puppet, see the Pharisee and the Tax Collector, Unit 6.

Books

What can we learn from story books written for under fives that will help us in our story telling?

Many writers for under 5s base their stories around the lives of children that age, their families and their immediate environment. For example, Shirley Hughes' stories are centred round the lives of a toddler brother and sister. She has a superb way of capturing the life and experience of the toddler in her books so that both children and parents can relate to the characters. In her book *Alfie's Feet* she tells the story of Alfie and his first Wellington boots. She starts by showing Alfie with his baby sister Annie and talking about how Alfie can walk but his sister can't quite yet. Alfie likes to splash through puddles, but this leaves his shoes and socks all wet. So his mother takes him

to buy a pair of boots, and as soon as he gets home, he tries them on and insists on going to the park. However the boots feel funny although they are "very smart and shiny".

Alfie looks down at his feet. They still feel funny.

They keep turning outwards.
Dad is sitting on a bench.
They both look at Alfie's feet.
Suddenly Alfie knows what is wrong.
He has his boots on the wrong feet! When they get home his mother paints a big L and R on the appropriate boots. In due course Annie gets a pair of boots of her own, too.

The story is very simple, and straightforward. But the pictures illustrating the story are not. They are full of detail and incident. When they go shopping Alfie takes his elephant with him. When they get back from shopping, Annie empties the shopping bag all over the floor and is seen trying to open a packet of biscuits. All of the elements are there for a child: activity, going places and things happening.

Shirley Hughes' books reach right into the child's world, the world of immediate family, of home, children's games and fantasies. They start with what is familiar to the child.

Books for toddlers often portray the special relationship between under 5s and their parents. This is one of the themes that comes up again and again in Jan Ormerod's books. *Messy Baby*, *Reading*, *Sleeping* all show a lively toddler chasing around, and on, under and over the parent. It is the child who is active, rather than the parent. As we look at these can we think of the special relationship that exists between us and our heavenly Father?

As we tell our own stories we have to start with what is familiar to the children and parents, and we need to involve them in what is hapening. We can draw our audience into the story by asking questions about the children and their lives, or by using bright illustrations and visual aids. This will add to the interest and help to keep everyone's attention.

The next time you discover a book which fascinates a child, ask what the "magic ingredients" are, and try to apply them to your own story telling.

When Jesus told parables people wanted to listen to what he had to say. He spoke in their language about things that were familiar to them, and he used this to point people to his heavenly Father.

Using the activity sheets

Read through the activity sheet well before you come to use it. This gives you time for forward planning (or you might find yourself having to collect 40 toilet rolls in a week...). The sheet itself has been divided up into four sections:
- You will need
- Prepare in advance
- Get the room ready
- What each child/parent does.

You will need
This lists all the material you will need for the activity. This is where it is most important to think ahead. Ask the parents in your group as well as other members of the church congregation.

Prepare in advance
You have now gathered together everything you need for a particular session. What next? This section talks about the specific things that you need to do to get the activity ready.

Use old cereal packets for your templates. They are cheap, and will withstand repeated drawing around. Splash out on a good pair of scissors, with long blades.

The individual preparation instructions are fairly straightforward. You will usually need one set of activity pieces per child, plus a few extra.

Once all the bits and pieces are cut out, group them together in separate bags to take to the session.

Make up an activity yourself before the session. It will help you to explain how to make it, and to have "one you made earlier" to show the group.

Get the room ready
The sheet will tell you what each child needs to make the activity. In the centre of the table put things like glue, spreaders, pencils, etc. You can use the lids from 2- or 4-litre ice cream tubs as trays for things. When you are using PVA glue put a small amount in a plastic (not glass) tub. If your tubs have lids you can keep it from session to session. With PVA glue, always use spreaders as brushes get all clogged up. Pritt might seem easier, but it doesn't stick so well. Once PVA is stuck, it is stuck. Make sure you have enough

glue spreaders to prevent children getting bored while they wait their turn.

If the activity needs sellotape, cut out the strips beforehand and stick them around an ice cream container lid. This avoids the need to have scissors out.

What each child/parent does
Show a completed activity to everybody, and explain one step at a time what you have to do to make one. Ask for questions, and be ready to help anyone with problems. (If you have a child under 3 it might be helpful to have someone looking after him or her while you explain it.)

Once the activity is made, ask mums or dads to write each child's name on the one they have made. They are often wet afterwards so leave them on the tables to dry.

Tidy up afterwards...
Have fun!

☞ *All measurements are given in cm (one inch is approximately 2.5 cm). Paper sizes (A2, 3, 4 and 5) follow the standard sizes.*

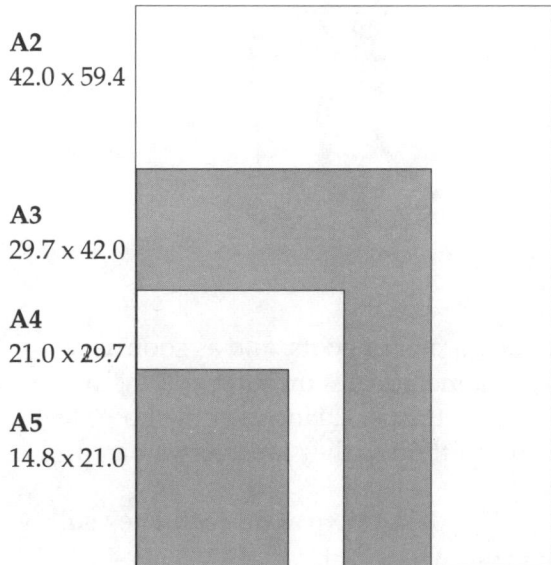

A2
42.0 x 59.4

A3
29.7 x 42.0

A4
21.0 x 29.7

A5
14.8 x 21.0

Everyone likes a good story, whatever their age and whatever century they live in. When Jesus was talking to the crowds he often used stories, or parables.

David Wenham, a Bible scholar, points out that "Jesus, especially when speaking to the crowds, spoke almost entirely pictorially, explaining his ideas in and through stories, and not just using stories to illustrate his point".

Jesus' stories reflected the world in which he lived. They were stories about family life, farming, weddings, and so on. His parables are as much for today as they were for Jesus' time, but we have to try to grasp the message and make the connection with our own world.

These ten units have been written with the world and experience of under 5s in mind. Some of the stories remain in their historical surrounding, and we have picked up a point where that world and the world of today meet; in others we have put the message across through a story that comes from our own children's world; further stories feature animals as leading characters.

We hope you enjoy using **Stories Jesus Told**. There is always something new for us to learn from Jesus' stories. Enjoy learning together!

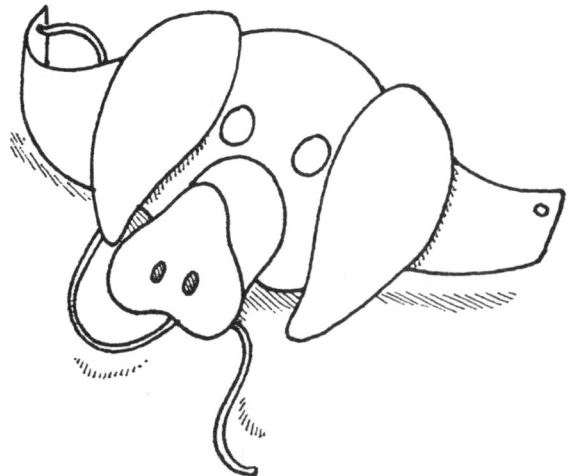

An invitation to a party

The Great Feast   *Luke 14:15-24*

When a child is going to a party there is a great deal of excitement in the house. Children look forward to these occasions with so much enthusiasm that it would be almost impossible to tell them that they couldn't go.

List the excuses in verses 18-20 that the people make to the invitation. What kind of excuses might people make today to turn down an invitation to find out more about Jesus?

Tell the story

❶ As the storyteller, you are playing the part of the servant. Introduce yourself and give yourself a name.

❷ The servant might start by saying something like: "My master is having a party and he has given me these invitations. Would some of you like to help me post them?"

❸ Ask a few of the children to help post the letters though the letter boxes.

❹ Continue by explaining about the party and getting things ready by putting up a few balloons and decorations. Ask the children to help lay the table, etc.

Theme
Jesus shows God's love

Let's sing!
❝ God's love is like a circle ❞
❝ Who's the king of the jungle? ❞
❝ 1-2-3 Jesus loves me ❞

Activity
Make crowns.

Visual aids
☆ 4-6 postcard invitations
☆ 4-6 large cardboard doors in different designs with letter boxes
☆ a table with 4-6 chairs, preferably child-sized, table cloth, cups, plates, a few cakes, balloons and decorations
☆ 4-6 crowns like the ones that the children will make

❺ When everyone has sat down again, say something like: "Everything is ready for the party but the only replies I have had have been excuses why people are not coming.

So none of the guests will be at the party. My master has told me to go out and find people to come, but I don't know where to look..."

❻ Continue as if a thought has come into your head: "Would you children like to come to the party? You would? That's great! Now I haven't enough hats for everyone. Let's make some more..."

☞ *This is a very good story and activity if you are starting a Mums and Toddlers group, or a new term. Make it into a reason to have a party!*

Extra activity
For a new group, or one with lots of new children and parents:

Cut out balloon shapes from card and write each child's name on it as they arrive. Pin these on to a wall display. It helps the new children and parents feel part of the group straightaway and is a good point of reference for the leaders for children's names.

Crowns

Prepare in advance

❶Divide each large sheet of card into three long equal strips. Each strip will make two crowns.

❷Draw a zigzag lengthwise along the strip. Don't make the zigzag too small or it will involve a lot of cutting.

❸Cut along the zigzag and you have two crown shapes.

You will need
☆ bright coloured card: an A2 sheet makes 6 crowns
☆ sticky paper
☆ sticky stars
☆ staplers
☆ pencils

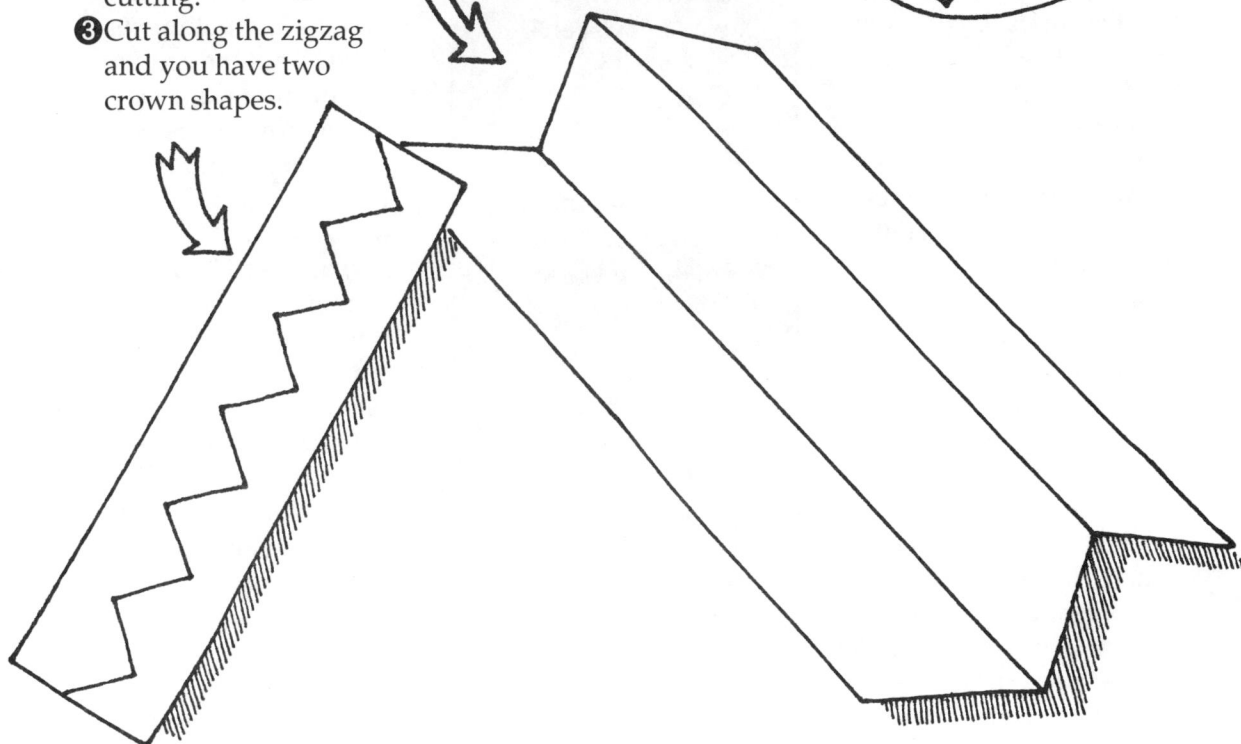

❹Cut the sticky paper into large circles, rectangles, triangles, squares, etc. Keep these about 2-4cm in diameter or length.

Get the room ready

Put out for each child/parent:
• 1 crown strip

Put out on the table:
• A selection of shapes and stars on a margarine tub lid or ice cream container lid
• staplers
• pencils

What each child/parent does

❶Stick the stars and shapes onto the crown.

❷Fold the crown round each child's head to measure the correct size.

❸Remove from the child's head and staple the ends of the crown together.

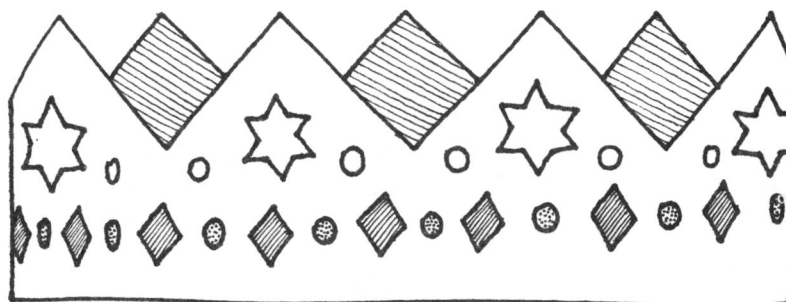

Activity Sheet – The Great Feast

The mustard seed

The Mustard Seed   *Mark 4:30-32*

Notice the detail that Jesus puts into this short Bible reference. In verse 31 he talks about where the seed is sown and in verse 32 about its size before and after it grows. Look again at verse 32 where we are told about life after it has grown to full size. In our story we have taken the image of the growing seed and applied it to the faith of children.

Tell the story

Introduction:
Start off by talking about big things, such as a big spoon or car, and small things, such as a small spoon or car. Explain that small things can grow into big ones. Find the smallest person in the room and the largest person. Get the parents and children to make themselves as small as possible, and then to grow bigger and bigger to introduce the idea of things growing.

Show the group a packet of seeds with a picture of the plant on the front. If you are doing this with a large group or in a church service you will probably have to make a seed packet out of an A4 size envelope and put a large picture on the front. Open the packet and put a seed on your hand. Point out that on the front of the packet there is a picture of a whole plant. Ask the group what has to happen

Theme
God wants our love for him to grow and grow

Let's sing!
" Have you seen the pussy cat? "
" God is for me, though I am little "
" Who made the twinkling stars? " (make up verses about sun and rain)

Activity
Make mustard and cress heads.

Visual aids
☆ examples of large and small things
☆ a packet of flower seeds
☆ a packet of mustard seeds
☆ a wall display of a growing mustard plant (see activity sheet for details)

for the seed to become a plant.

Story:
Build up your visual aid as you tell each stage of the story.

- Jesus told a story about a farmer who planted some seeds. (Your visual aid should show some brown card to represent the soil at the bottom.)

- The farmer took some mustard seeds, the smallest seeds in the world, and planted them.
- He came back a few days later to find a little green shoot poking its head out of the ground.
- It grew more and more.
- The farmer came back again and found that the leaves were opening.
- "I thank God," said the farmer, "for the sun which gives light and warmth to help the plant grow."
- Another day when it was raining hard, the farmer looked out and saw his plant growing. "I thank God," he said, "for the rain. It gives the plant water to drink, and helps it take in minerals so it grows up strong and healthy."
- So as the weeks went past the farmer's plant grew and grew. (Ask the children to help the plant grow by sticking on the branches.)
- After a while the tiny seed grew into the biggest plant of all. Its branches were so big that the birds came and built their nests there.
- Although we might only be little, we can love Jesus, and that is what he wants us to do. Then as we grow he wants us to learn to love him more and more.

Mustard and cress heads

You will need

☆ I egg shell per child
☆ half a toilet roll tube per child
☆ green sticky paper
☆ scraps of coloured card for bow tie
☆ 8mm sticky dots
☆ damp cotton wool balls
☆ a packet of mustard and cress seeds
☆ pencils
☆ PVA glue and spreaders

What each child/parent does

❶ Cover the toilet roll tube with sticky paper.
❷ Stick the dots on to the bow tie.
❸ Glue bow tie on to the toilet roll tube.

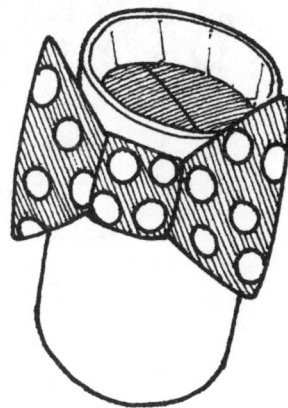

Prepare in advance

❶ Arrange for a number of families to collect used size 2 egg shells. It is best if the ends are broken off so that about two thirds of the shell is intact. Bring them in egg boxes, making sure you allow for breakages.
❷ Cut the toilet roll tubes in half. Cut the green sticky paper into strips about 15cm by 5cm to cover the tube.
❸ Cut out the bow template and cut out bows in assorted coloured scrap card. Cut sticky dots into strips of 7 dots.

Get the room ready

Put out for each child/parent:
• half a toilet roll
• 1 strip of green sticky paper
• 1 bow tie
• 1 set of dots

Put out on the table:
• egg shells standing in egg boxes with damp cotton wool inside them
• some mustard and cress seeds in small pots
• pencils
• glue and spreaders

❹ Write child's name on tube.
❺ Take egg shell and very carefully draw on face.
❻ Put egg shell into the top of the toilet roll.
❼ Sprinkle some seeds on to the damp cotton wool. The mustard and cress seeds will grow into "hair" for the egg shell "person". The children and parents must water the cotton wool to keep it from drying out, while taking care not to drown it. It will also need warmth and light. How about having mustard and cress sandwiches in a couple of weeks time?!

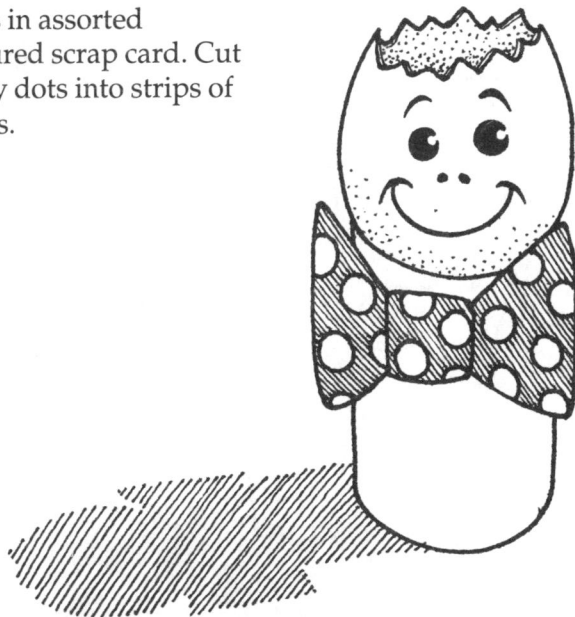

Activity Sheet – The Mustard Seed

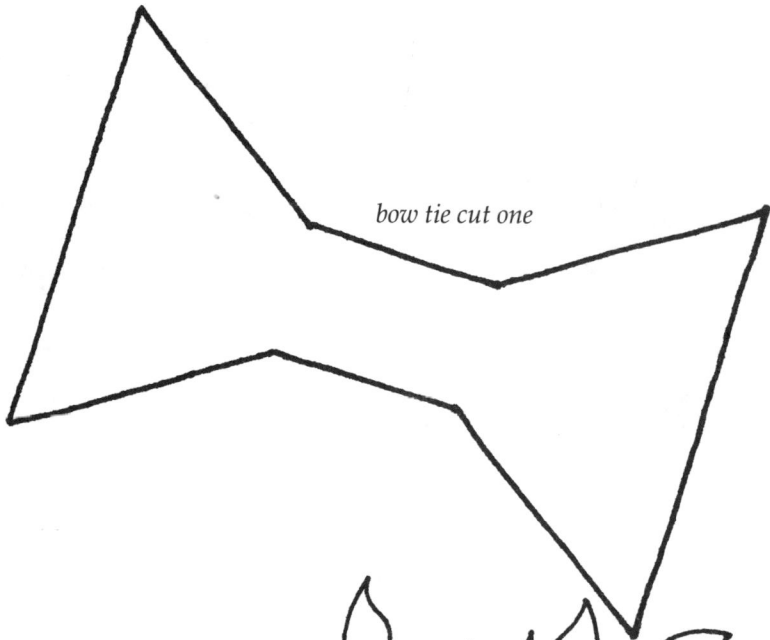

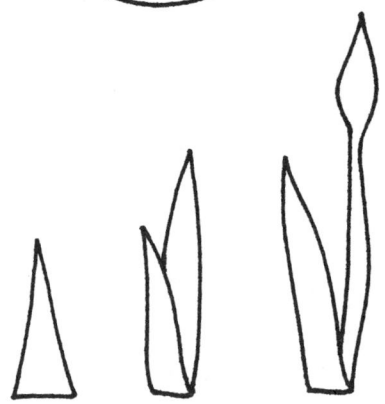

Template – The Mustard Seed

bow tie cut one

add branches

build up plant

A sheep is missing

The Lost Sheep   *Luke 15:4-7*

Jesus often tells stories with a particular group of people in mind. Who is he telling this story to according to verses 1-2? Look at verse 4 to see how important it is to the shepherd to find his lost sheep. What does verse 5 tell us about what the shepherd wants to do? In what way is Jesus like the shepherd according to verse 7?

Tell the story

Introduction:
Set out your assortment of containers with the duplo person hidden among them. Use the names of the children in the group to make a lost-and-found game: Pippa has lost her duplo figure. Can you help her find it? Use words like in, on, under and behind. Ask a child to come and help: "Darren, is it under the large green bucket?" Encourage the older or less shy children to look first so that the others get the hang of the game. Build up the suspense until the figure is found. The whole group will be pleased that the figure is safely back in Pippa's pocket.

Theme
God loves each and every one of us

Let's sing!
" Jesus' love is very wonderful "
" God is good, we sing and shout it "
" I was lost but Jesus found me "

Activity
Make a toilet roll sheep or sock puppet sheep.

Visual aids
☆ brightly coloured buckets and boxes in different shapes and sizes
☆ a duplo person
☆ 5 A3 or larger pictures with flaps

Helpful resources
" The Lost Sheep "
" Where's Spot? "
" The Lost Sheep: The Wonderful Stories of Jesus " New Testament Book 1

✎ *Notes* _____

_____

_____

_____

_____

_____

_____

_____

The Lost Sheep

stick on tab

lift up flap

No

stick on tab

No

fold over flap

A3 sheets

Story:

❶ Tell the story of the lost sheep very simply in your own words, using the lift-the-flap pictures to help. These should be A3 sheets with a cut out picture of a rock or bush stuck on to a tab at the top. Four of the flaps will have nothing beneath them while one will have a picture of a sheep.

❷ When working out the story write down the different stages:
- introduce the shepherd and his 100 sheep
- 1 sheep goes missing

- use the 5 lift-the-flap pictures to illustrate where the shepherd might look for his sheep - behind the rock, in the ditch, under the bush, over the cliff, stuck in a stream, lifting up the flaps so the children can answer "No," until it is found in picture 5
- the shepherd celebrates finding his sheep by having a party
- Jesus loves each one of us just as much as the shepherd loved his sheep

☞ *You might like to encourage the parents to play a similar game at home, hiding the sheep made in the activity, using words like in, on, under, behind, etc.*

Sheep: 1

Prepare in advance
1. Cut out templates for face, ears and eyes, inner and outer.
2. Cut out face in black felt.
3. Cut out ears in black felt.
4. Cut out outer eyes in white felt.
5. Cut out inner eyes in black felt.
6. Stick the inner eyes on to the outer eyes. If you use a black marker pen to draw on the inner eyes you won't need the black felt inner eyes.

Get the room ready
Put out for each child/parent:
- 1 white sock
- 1 set of felt pieces
Put out on the table:
- glue and spreaders
- scraps of paper
- pencils to write on the child's name

What each child/parent does
1. Put sock on to child's hand.
2. Glue on the sheep features.

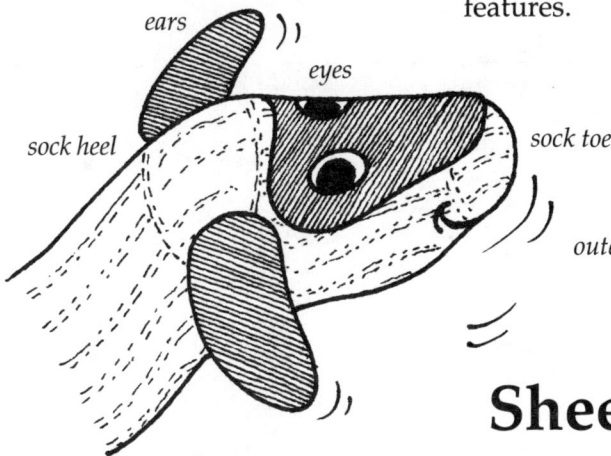

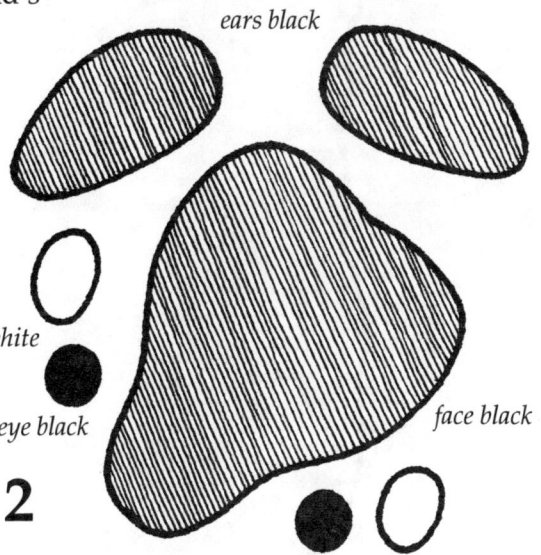

You will need
☆ old white or nearly white socks, child size 2-7, preferably thick
☆ black and white pieces of felt
☆ material glue such as Copydex and spreaders

ears

eyes

sock heel

sock toe

ears black

outer eye white

inner eye black

face black

Sheep: 2

You will need
☆ white card: 1 A2 sheet makes 6 sheep
☆ toilet roll tubes: 1 per sheep
☆ PVA glue and spreaders
☆ pencils
☆ black crayons

Get the room ready
Put out for each child/parent:
- 1 sheep body
- 1 sheep head
- 1 sheep tail
- 1 toilet roll tube
Put out on the table:
- PVA glue and spreaders
- black crayons
- pencils

What each child/parent does
1. Fold the sheep body around the toilet roll and stick down the 2 flaps marked A. The sheep should now stand on its 4 legs.
2. Draw the face on the face card, with eyes, nose, ears and mouth.
3. Fold up flap B on the sheep body and stick on the back of the head.
4. Colour the feet black.
5. Stick on tail.

Prepare in advance
1. Cut out the templates for sheep's face, body and tail in scrap card or an old cereal packet.
2. Cut out in white card the number of faces, bodies and tails required.

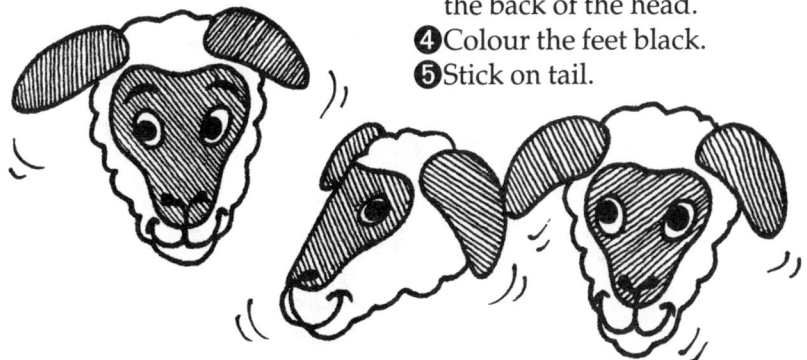

Activity Sheet – The Lost Sheep

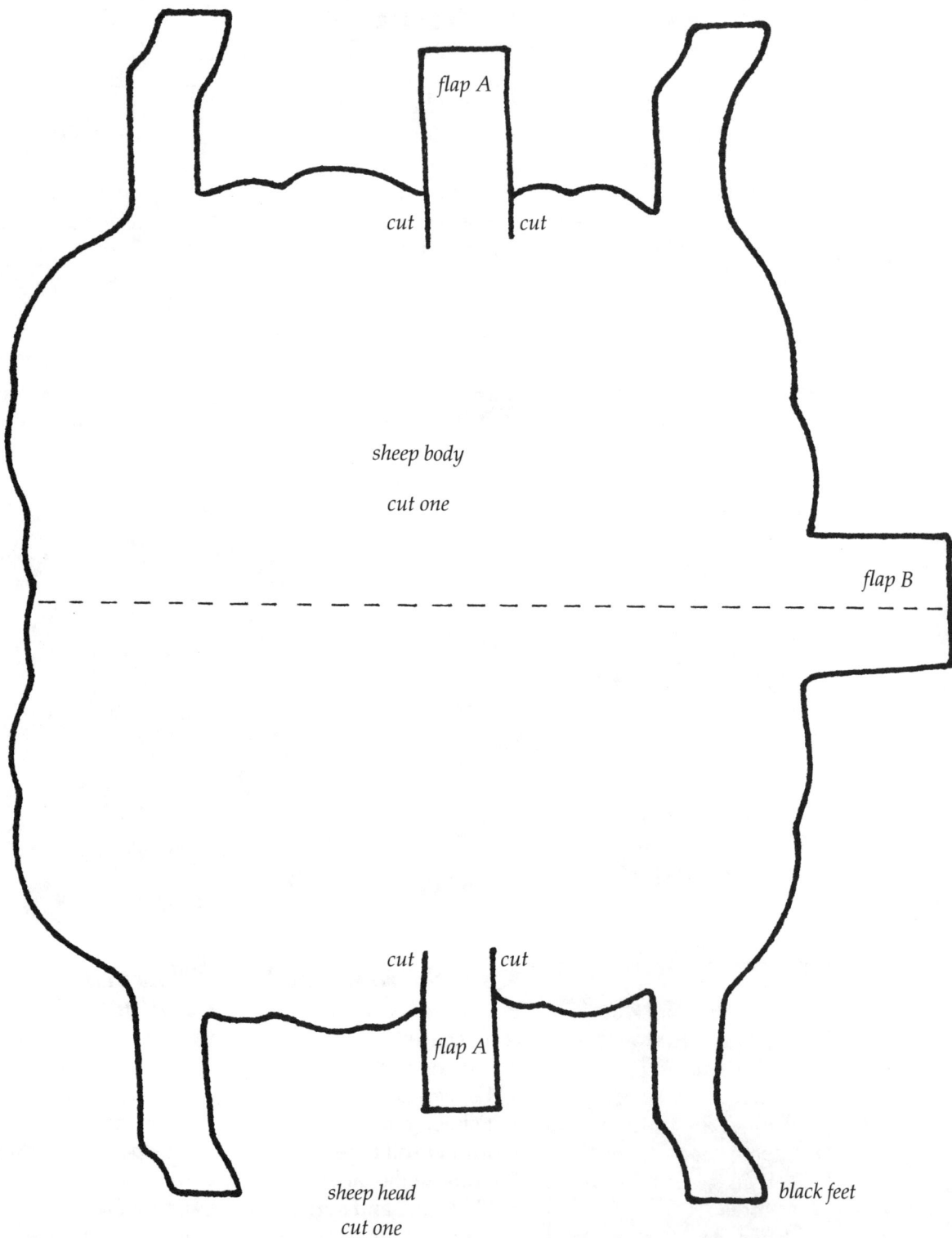

Template – The Lost Sheep

flap A

cut   cut

sheep body

cut one

flap B

cut   cut

flap A

sheep head

cut one

black feet

sheep tail

cut one

The lost coin

The Lost Coin   *Luke 15:8-10*

Imagine how you would feel if, while hanging out the washing one day, you discovered that you had lost the stone from a ring that is very precious to you. All of the things that you had done that morning would flash through your mind: taking the children to playgroup, peeling the vegetables, cleaning the bathroom. Look in verse 8 to see what this woman did. How do you think she felt? Notice her reaction to finding the coin in verse 9.

Tell the Story

Introduction:
The storyteller is looking under, behind and in things, turning out her pockets and so on to find her lost ring. When she finds it she is overjoyed! The children could help with the search, as if playing hunt the thimble.

Story:
❶ Explain that today's story is about a lady

Theme
Jesus celebrates when he finds we're his friends

Let's sing!
- " Lord, you gave me joy in my heart "
- " Stand up, clap hands "
- " I have hands "

Activity
Make a headdress of coins.

Visual aids
- ☆ a 10-coin headdress with one missing
- ☆ a broom
- ☆ a scarf or material for headwear
- ☆ a wedding or engagement ring

---

who has lost something very important and you are going to play the part of the lady. Give yourself a name. Put on the scarf and coin headdress. Tell the children (and parents) that the silver coin headdress is like a wedding ring, given to the bride on her wedding day.

❷ Tell the story very simply, in your own words, with actions. You will probably have the following steps: the coin goes missing; you search for the coin, sweeping around the house, looking carefully and thoroughly behind things; you find the lost coin; you put the coin back on to the headdress (use double-sided sticky tape or tie the ribbon in an easy bow so that you can slip the coin back on); show the joy and happiness of the lady at finding her coin.

❸ Jesus celebrates, just like the lady (use the name) in the story, when we want to be his friends and to follow him.

✎ *Notes* _____

_____

_____

_____

_____

_____

_____

_____

Coin headdress

> **Y**ou will need
> ☆ flattened silver
>   milk bottle tops
> ☆ thin ribbon
> ☆ hole punch

Prepare in advance
❶ Punch 2 holes in each milk bottle top to prevent the tops grouping up on the ribbon.
❷ Cut the ribbon into lengths between 60 and 80cm.

Get the room ready
Put out for each child/parent:
• 1 piece of ribbon
• 10 milk bottle tops

What each child/parent does
Thread the ribbon through the holes in the tops and tie the ribbon to the required length around the child's head. (A knot is better than a bow.)

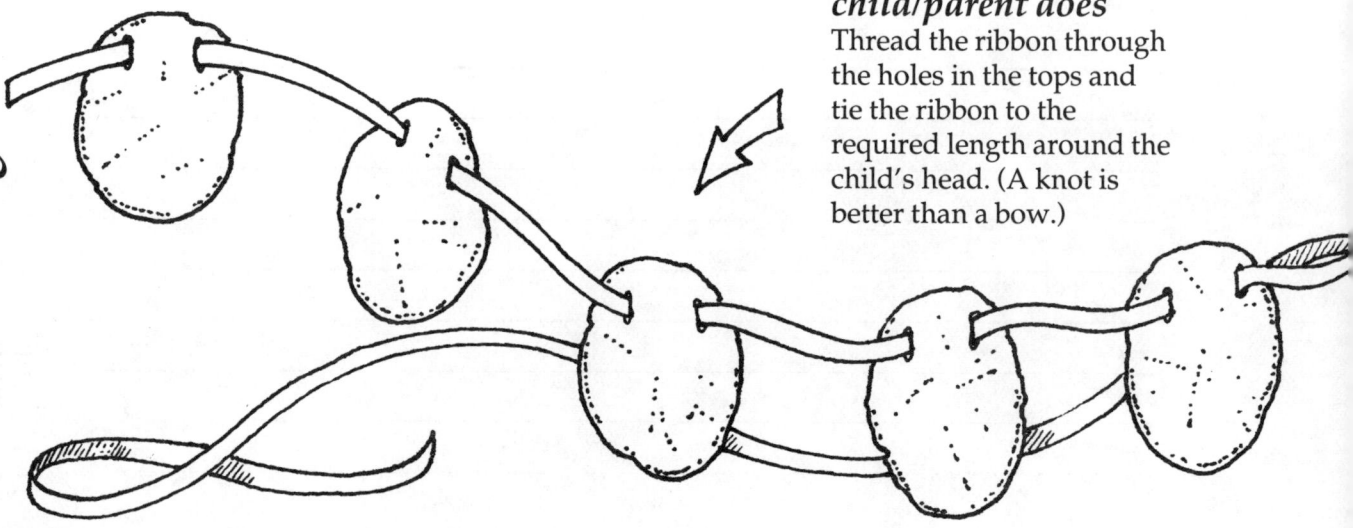

The father who forgave

The Lost Son   *Luke 15:11-31*

When you have a friend and you do something that hurts or upsets them, you have to say sorry before your friendship can be put right. This story is about a son who hurts his father. Look at verse 17 to see what a state the son was in before he saw what he had done. For a relationship to be fully restored, one has to forgive and one has to be forgiven. In verses 20-24 we read how the father reacts when he sees his son.

Tell the story

Introduction:
Play a game of "Simon says": Simon says clap your hands, stamp your feet, etc. The children have to copy the leader only when he or she says "Simon says". Don't aim to find a winner, but incorporate into the game actions and sounds from the story, like waving goodbye, rubbing tummy, pig sounds, etc.

Story:
❶ Introduce the father and his two sons. One of the sons leaves home with his money to have a good time with his "friends". But when his money has all gone, his friends all go too. He ends up hungry and the only job he can find is

---

Theme
God loves us, even when we do wrong

Let's sing!
" Thank you, Lord: " tune "Thank you, Lord, for this fine day": make up verses about things appropriate to the children
" Have you seen the pussycat? "
" God is for me "

Activity
Make pig masks.

Visual aids
☆ faces on stick puppets: a son, with a happy and a sad side; father; brother; crowd; and a collection of pigs - make the faces child size and stick them onto garden sticks
☆ a bag of money

Helpful resources
" The Son Who Came Back: The Wonderful Stories of Jesus " New Testament Book 1

---

looking after pigs. Eventually he decides to go home and say that he is sorry. He arrives home where there is great excitement in his father's house. His father forgives him, although his brother is a bit grumpy about it. The father explains that the son he had lost has been found.
❷ Make sure that you work out when to use the puppets.
❸ Involve the children in the story by having

them wave goodbye to the son as he goes, rubbing their tummies when he is hungry, making the pig noises and so on. Use your imagination. Mark the noises on to your notes. Remember you are telling the story, not reading it.

☞ *Be careful not to make this too complicated: the main point has to do with the father's forgiveness.*

Activity Sheet – The Lost Son

Pig masks

Prepare in advance

1. Cut out pig templates.
2. Cut out pig faces. For a child under 3 use eye position Y, over 3 use position Z.
3. Put in holes at X points, using hole punch.
4. Cut out both parts of snout.
5. Cut out 1 pair of ears per pig mask.
6. Cut elastic into lengths of about 30cm to go round the back of child's head.
7. Cut toilet roll tubes in half across.

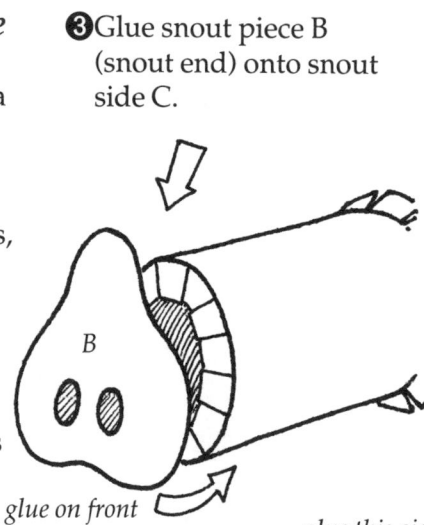

Get the room ready

Put out for each child/parent:

- a pig face
- both snout pieces
- a pair of ears
- a length of elastic
- half a toilet roll tube
- elastic band

Put out on the table:

- PVA glue and spreaders
- black crayon and pencils

What each child/parent does

1. Take snout piece A and wrap around toilet roll tube. Hold in place with elastic band.
2. Fold side C of snout in, and side D out. (This can be done as part of the preparation if preferred.)

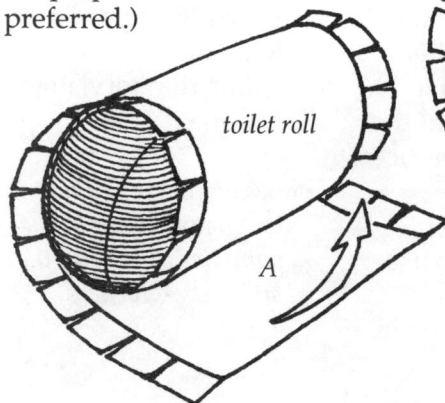

3. Glue snout piece B (snout end) onto snout side C.

glue on front

4. Glue around D side of snout, attach to back of nose and stick on to face.

glue this side of D

wrong side of pig mask

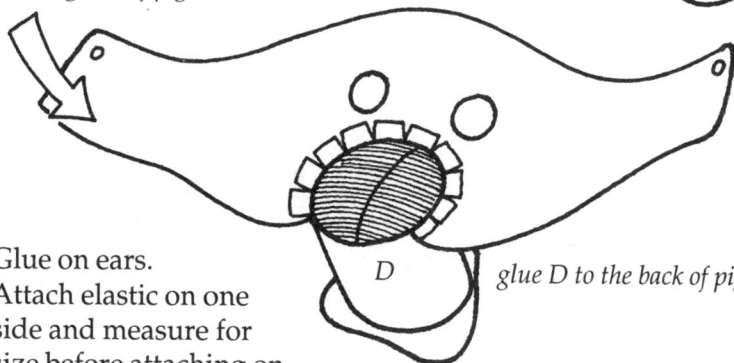

glue D to the back of pig mask

5. Glue on ears.
6. Attach elastic on one side and measure for size before attaching on to the second side.

attach elastic

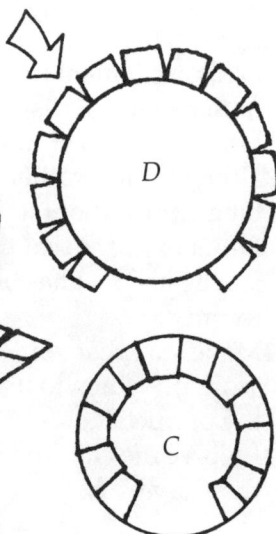

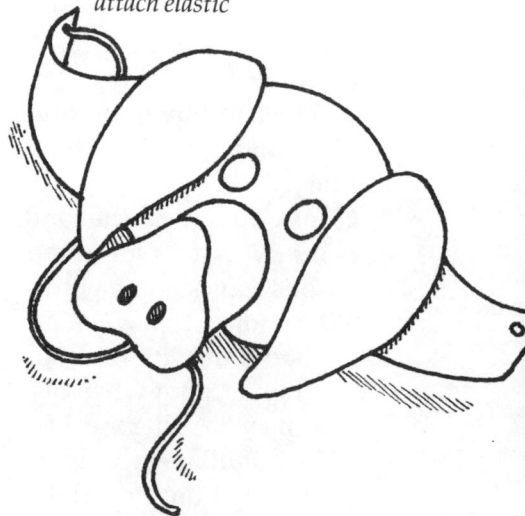

toilet roll

You will need

- ☆ pink card: 1 A2 sheet makes 4 pig masks
- ☆ toilet roll tubes
- ☆ elastic 6mm wide
- ☆ hole punch
- ☆ black crayon
- ☆ PVA glue and glue spreaders
- ☆ pencils
- ☆ small elastic bands

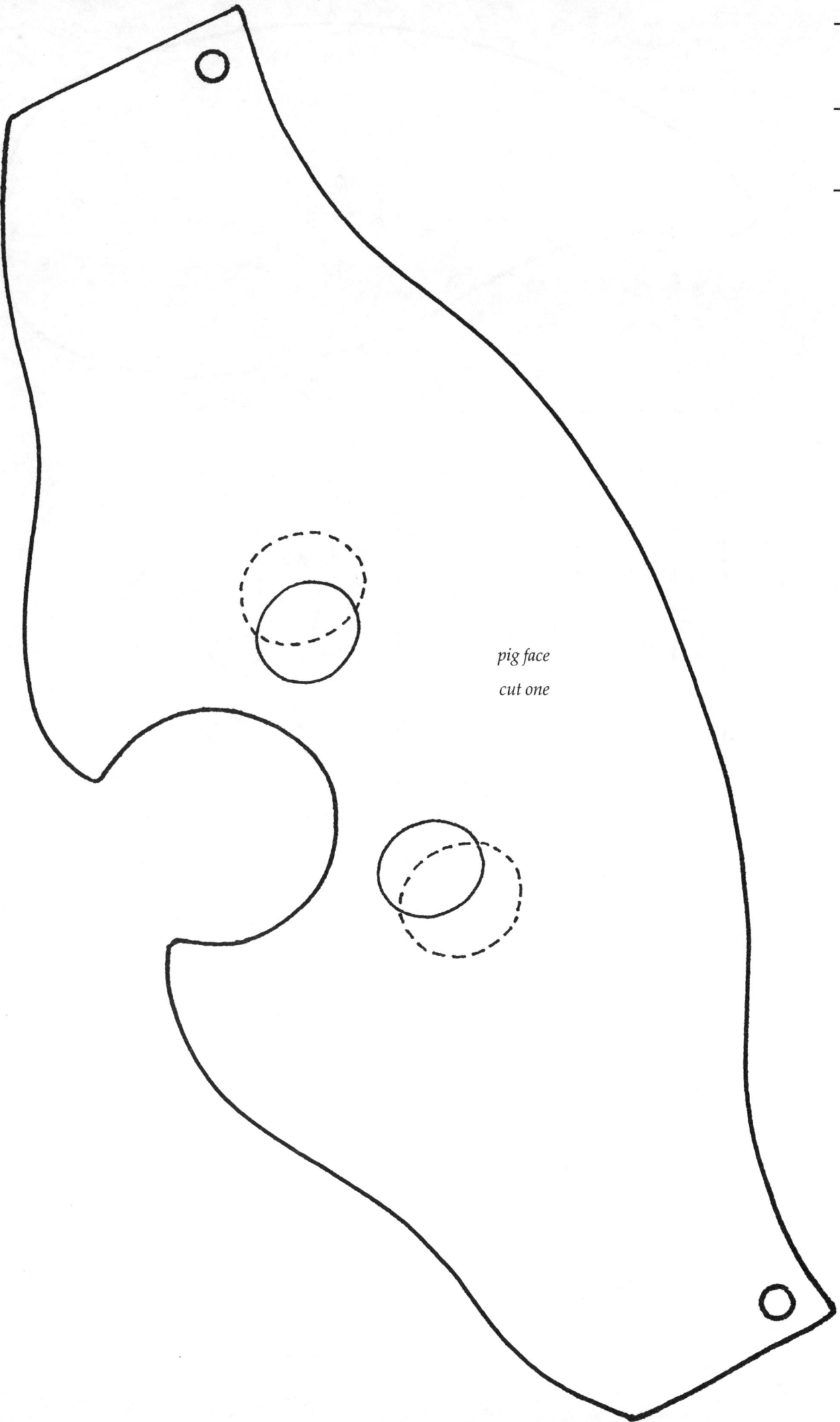

pig face

cut one

Template – The Lost Son

Template – The Lost Son

pig's ear cut two

side C   side D

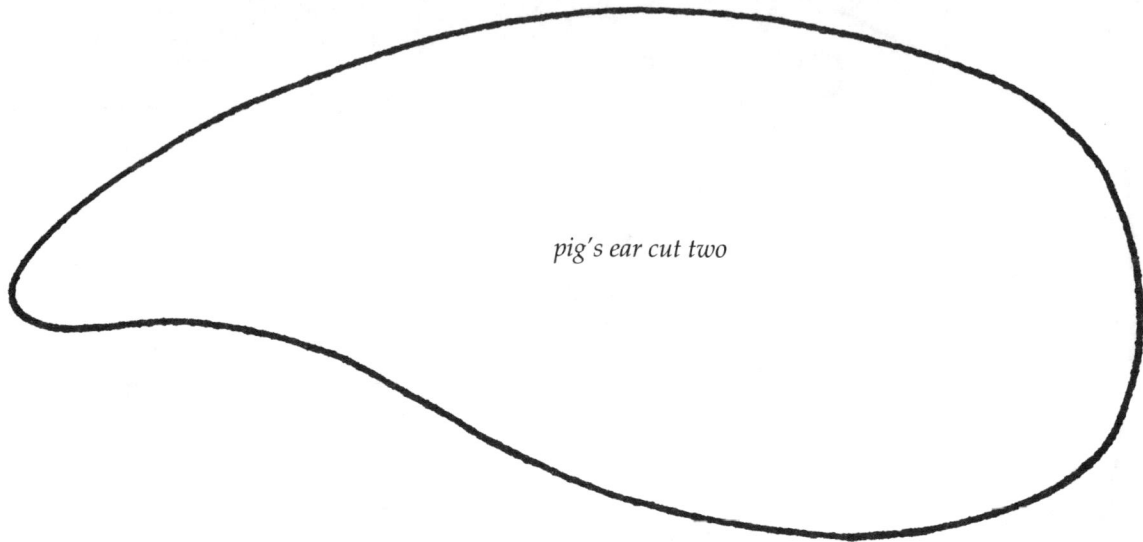

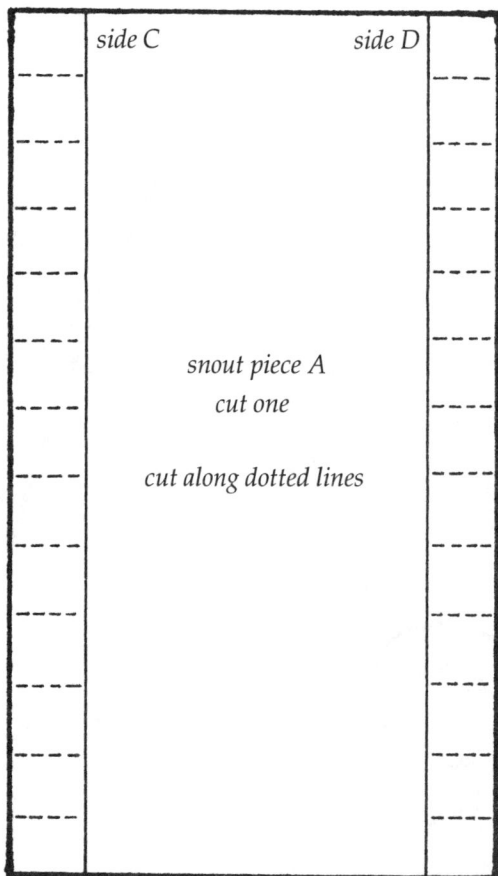

snout piece B
cut one

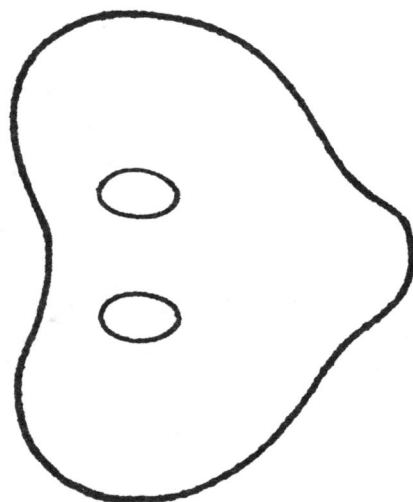

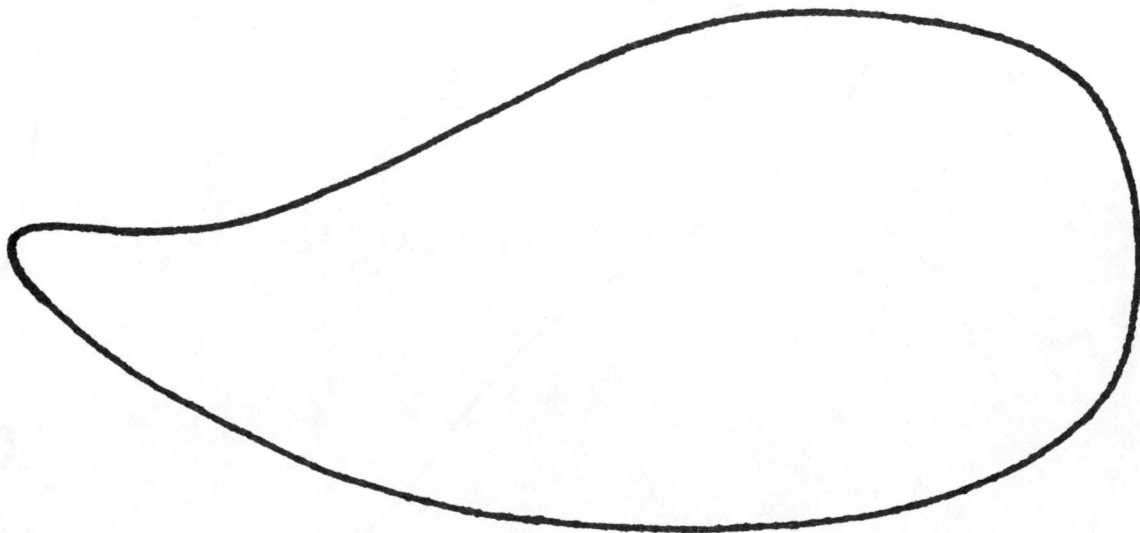

snout piece A
cut one

cut along dotted lines

The Pharisee and the tax collector

The Pharisee and the Tax Collector

Luke 18:9-14

giggling

happy

bored

glum

sad

angry

Theme
Jesus shows us
how to pray

Let's sing!
❝ God is for me ❞
❝ God is good, we
sing and shout it ❞
❝ Two little eyes to
look to God ❞

Activity
Make a happy and
sad face badge.

Visual aids
☆ basic face on a
stick puppet with
giggling, happy,
bored, sad, glum
and angry faces on
them (see page 4)
☆ a Pharisee and a
tax collector
puppet (see page
24)

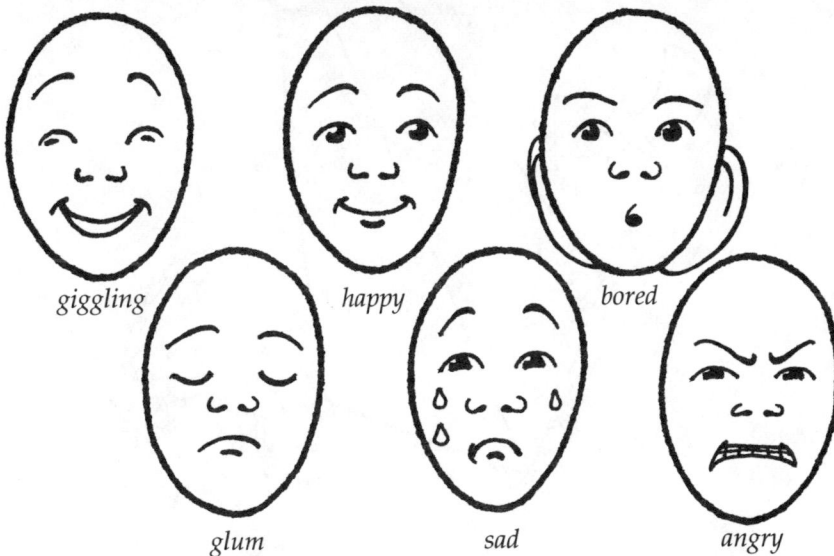

Jesus compares two people and their attitudes to God in this story. Look at verse 9 to see why Jesus told this story. What does verse 14 tell us about the Pharisee's mistake: was he wrong to give thanks? What does the same verse tell us that God requires in prayer?

Tell the story

Introduction:
Show the faces on sticks one at a time and ask what expressions the faces show. Talk about the feeling being shown on the faces. Get the children and parents to make the faces themselves!

Story

❶ Call your Pharisee puppet Harold, and explain that he is part of a very religious group of people.

❷ One day he went to pray in the Temple (which was like a church) and Harold stood, as usual, in the middle where everyone could see him. And in a big voice he prayed (use a big voice) "I thank you, God, that I am not like everybody else. I am not unfair. I help people, and I give some of my money away to charity. Haven't I been good? And I thank you that I'm not like that man over there."

❸ "Over there" is a tax collector. Call him Pete and explain how tax collectors were not very popular because sometimes they would cheat and take too much money from people. In the Temple he stood at the back, right in a corner, looking at the floor, and in a quiet voice he prayed (use a quiet voice) "Please

forgive me, God. I am sorry for all of the wrong things that I have done."

❹ Jesus said that it was Pete, the tax collector, whom God was pleased with that day, not the Pharisee.

❺ Finish off by saying that it is important for us to say sorry to God and to thank him properly for all of the good things that he gives us.

Pharisee and tax collector puppets

You will need:
- 2 A4 sheets of purple card, or any rich colour
- 1 A4 sheet of grey card
- 2 A4 sheets of white card

Tax Collector:

❶ Fold a sheet of grey card in half lengthwise. Mark 5cm along the top and 10cm along the bottom. Join up these two points.

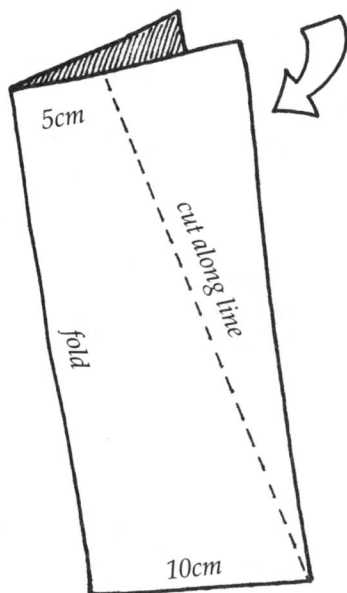

5cm

fold

cut along line

10cm

❷ Cut along the line while the card is folded. This shape makes the body.

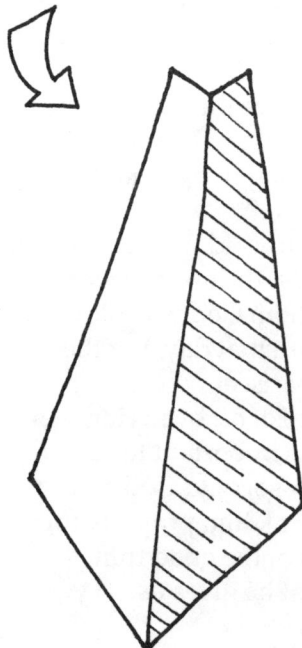

❸ Draw two heads as shown below. In white card cut out the head, draw on the face and colour in the hair. Stick the head on to the grey body.

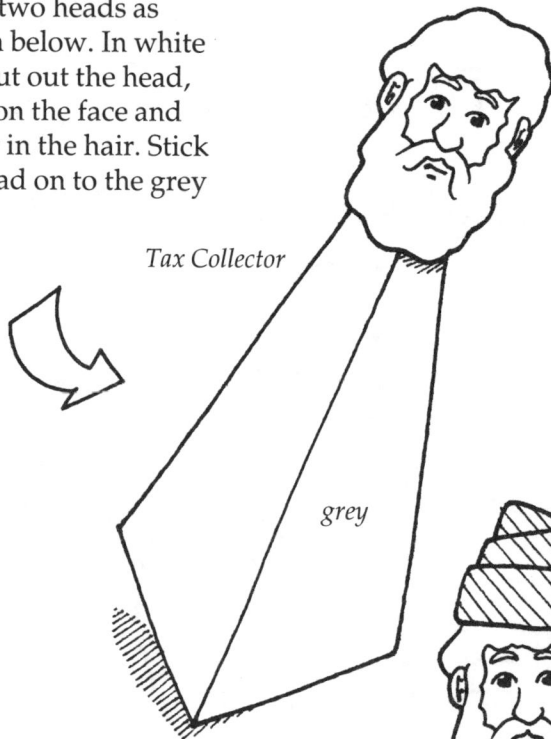

Tax Collector

grey

Pharisee:

❹ Repeat steps 1-3 for the Pharisee, using the purple card for the body. Try to make the face different.

❺ Draw a hat as shown below. Cut out the hat in purple card and put it on the Pharisee's head.

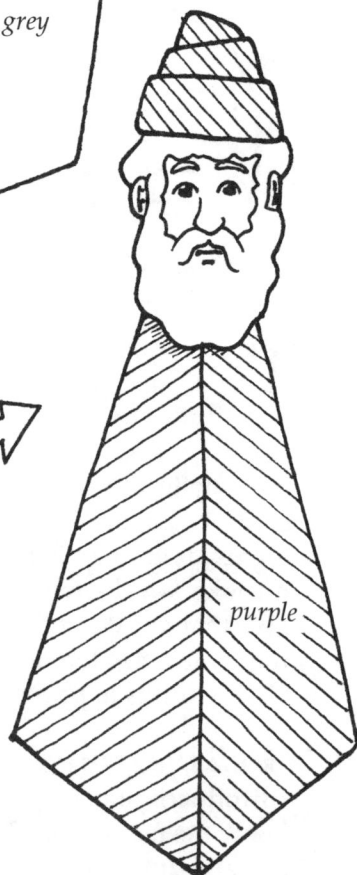

purple

Pharisee

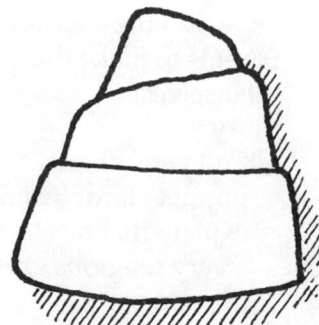

The happy and sad face badge

Prepare in advance

❶ Cut out cardboard templates of the two face circles, mouths, eyes and hair.

❷ In white card, cut out for each face both the face circles. With the bradawl, make a hole in the centre of each circle.

❸ Cut out the back of the badge in thick white card, put a hole through it with the bradawl, and stick on the safety pin using sticky tape, making sure that the tape does not cover the hole.

❹ Cut out hair in the coloured sticky paper.

You will need

☆ white card: an A2 sheet makes 10 badges
☆ black, brown or yellow sticky paper
☆ split pins
☆ safety pins
☆ thick white card
☆ strong tape
☆ pencils
☆ crayons
☆ a bradawl, or something to make holes with

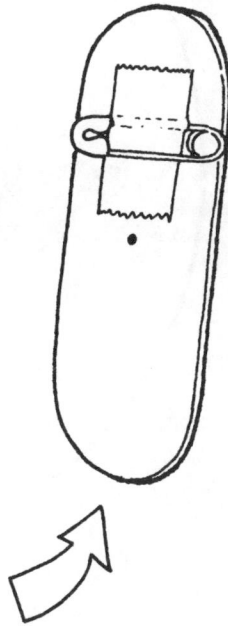

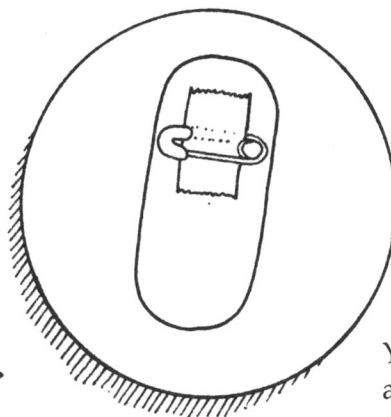

Get the room ready

Put out for each child/parent:
• 1 badge back with pin attached
• the two face circles
• hair

Put out on the table:
• pencils and crayons

What each child/parent does

❶ Take both the face circles and place A on B. Put them both on the badge back. Push the split pin through all three holes and fold it out at the back.

❷ Draw in two round eyes and a happy mouth. Rotate circle B through 90°. Draw in sad, half-circle eyes and sad mouth.

❸ Rotate circle B through another 90°. Draw in happy eyes and a happy mouth.

❹ Rotate circle B through another 90° and draw in sleepy eyes and a sleepy mouth.

❺ Stick on hair.

❻ Write on name.

You now have a happy and sad face badge, and when you go to bed you can make it go to sleep as well.

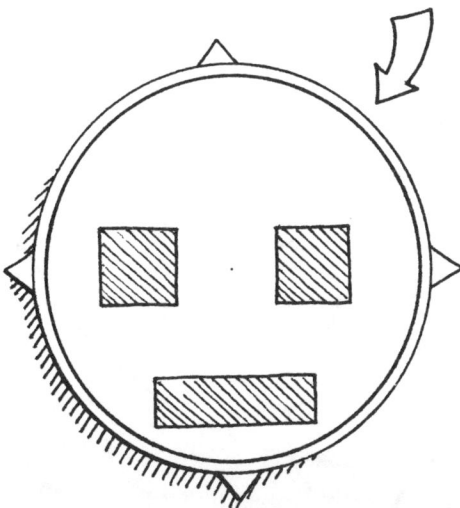

Activity Sheet – The Tax Collector

Template – The Tax Collector

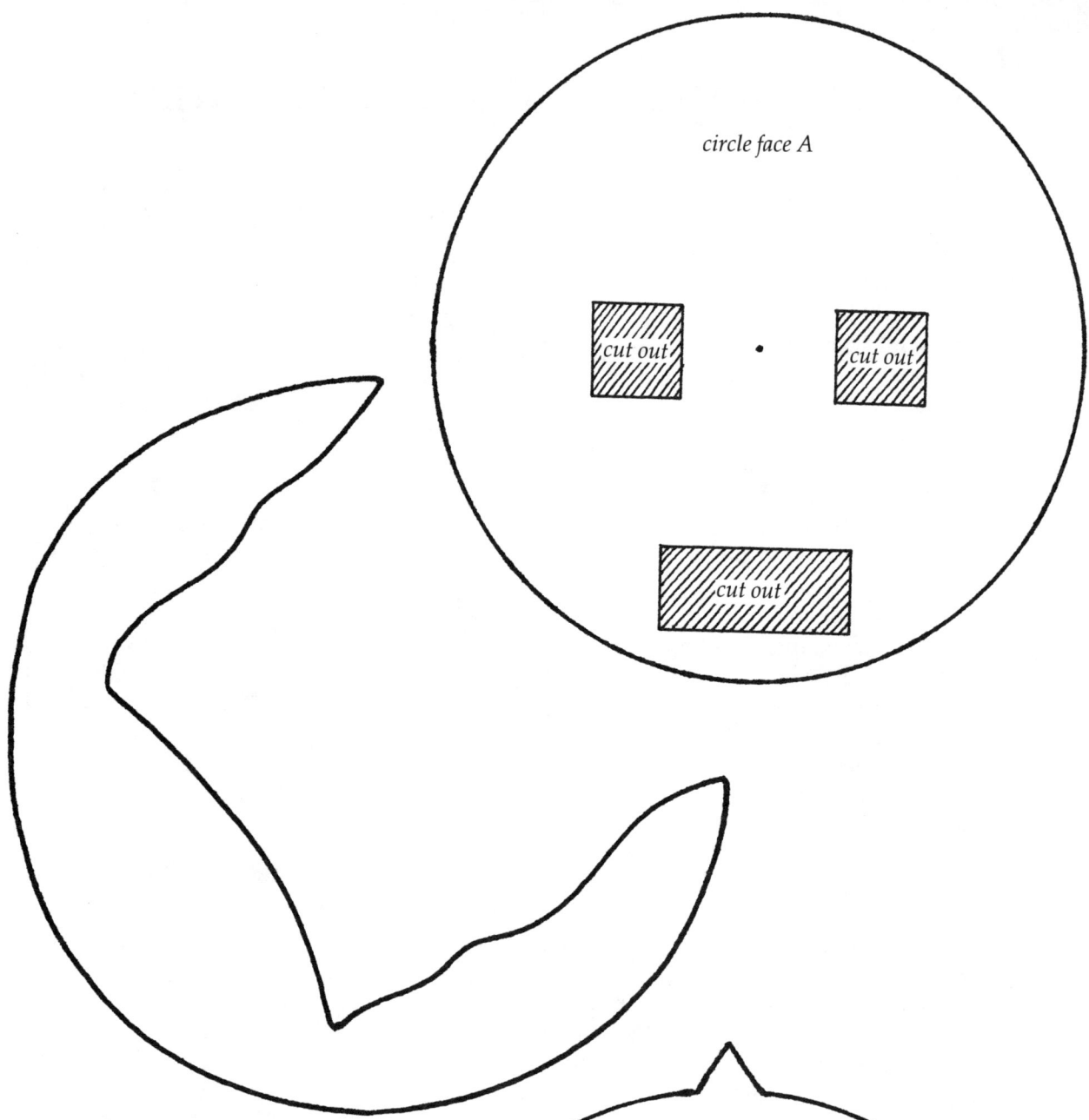

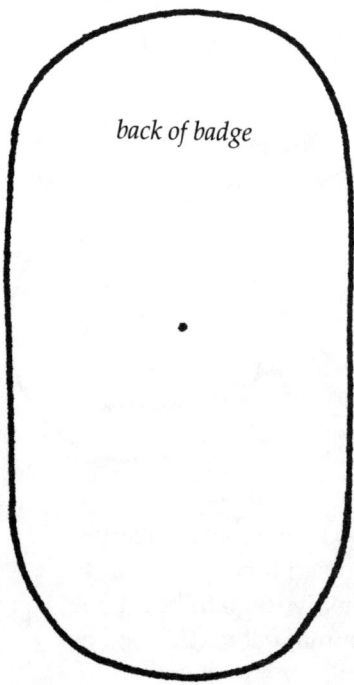

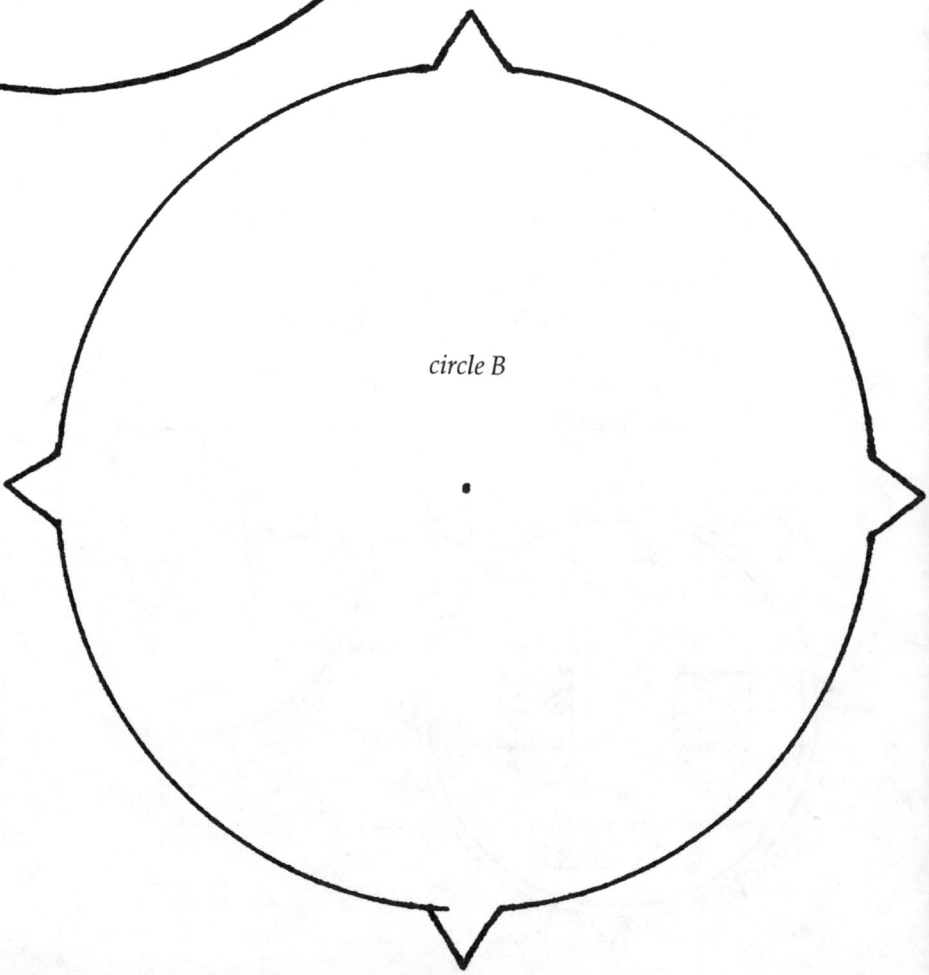

circle face A

cut out

cut out

cut out

back of badge

circle B

The two brothers

The Two Sons   *Matthew 21:28-32*

Jesus tells a story about two brothers who say one thing, but do another. Look at verses 29 and 30 for the immediate response of each to his father's request and for what each brother actually did. How would you feel if you were the father? As you read the story written here look back at the Bible text and see how the two fit together.

Tell the story
Introduction:
Ask the children what jobs they help with around the house. Have a collection of props to help illustrate them, e.g. washing up bowl and cloth, box with some toys, dustpan and brush, mixing bowl and wooden spoon, basket of clothes. If someone tells you a job that you haven't got a prop for, try to use it in the song.

After you have done this for a few minutes sing "Here we go round the mulberry bush", substituting three or four jobs for the original words, and using actions. For example, "This is the way we clean the car, clean the car, clean the car. This is the way we clean the car on a cold and frosty morning."
Story:
This is a retelling of the parable of the two sons. Write these steps into direct speech and learn them so that you can tell it

Theme
Jesus says what we do is more important than what we promise

Let's sing!
- " I have hands "
- " Jesus' love is very wonderful "
- " I'm glad I live in a house "

Activity
Make two finger-leg puppets.

Visual aids
☆ two toddler puppets (see Book 1 for instructions), both wearing jumpers and trousers, and one wearing wellies
☆ a dad puppet
☆ old green or brown towel or piece of carpet to represent the garden
☆ bits of dead leaves and twigs
☆ a basket or box to collect the garden rubbish in
☆ props for "Here we go round the mulberry bush"

Helpful resources
- " The Lion Book of Bible Stories and Prayers " (section 7)
- " The Two Sons "

as an exciting story.
❶ Give the two brothers names, e.g. Matthew and Daniel.
❷ Dad asks Daniel to help him to sweep up the dead leaves and the weeds.
❸ Daniel says that he is too busy playing with his cars and garage. But after his dad has gone he realizes that he can play with them any time, so puts on his wellies and goes out into the garden to help.
❹ Dad finds Matthew watching TV and asks

him to help.
❺ Matthew says that he will and he'll just go and put on his wellies.
❻ Daniel is brushing up the leaves when his dad arrives and soon the two of them have finished. Matthew is still watching the television.
❼ Who has made his dad happy, Daniel or Matthew?

The answer is Daniel. Saying we will do things isn't enough; we have to do things as well.

Two brothers - finger-leg puppets

Prepare in advance

❶ Cut out cardboard templates for the boys' bodies, jumpers, faces, hair, broom, hand.

❷ In blue or green card cut out the boys (two for each child).

❸ In flesh coloured sticky paper cut out faces and hands.

❹ Cut out hair in black, brown or yellow sticky paper so that each boy has different coloured hair.

❺ Using the old catalogues or magazines, cut out pictures of jumpers and cut them to size for the boys. This gives a good texture to the boys' clothes, but if these are not available, use brightly coloured paper.

❻ Cut out the broom in brown card.

Get the room ready

Put out for each child/parent:
- brother A
- brother B
- face A
- face B
- hair A
- hair B
- jumper A
- jumper B
- broom A
- hand B

Put out on the table:
- PVA glue and spreaders
- pencils

What each child/parent does

❶ Stick face, hair, jumper and broom on brother A. Draw on face features.

❷ Stick face, hand, hair and jumper on brother B. Draw on face features.

❸ Write on the names of the puppets.

You will need

☆ blue or green card: A2 sheet makes 8 sets of puppets

☆ flesh coloured sticky paper

☆ black, brown or yellow sticky paper

☆ old clothes catalogues or brightly coloured paper

☆ scraps of brown card

☆ PVA glue and spreaders

❹ To make them walk, put your index and middle finger through the holes, one puppet per hand.

☞ If you are working with younger children, you might decide only to make one puppet, puppet A.

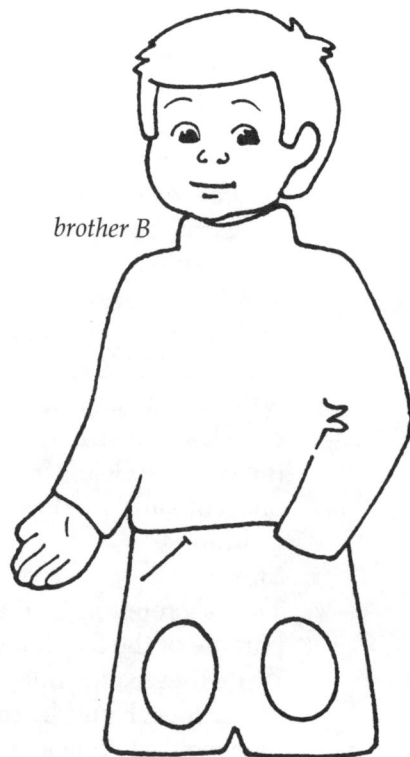

brother A

brother B

brother B
body

hair

hand

jumper

head/face

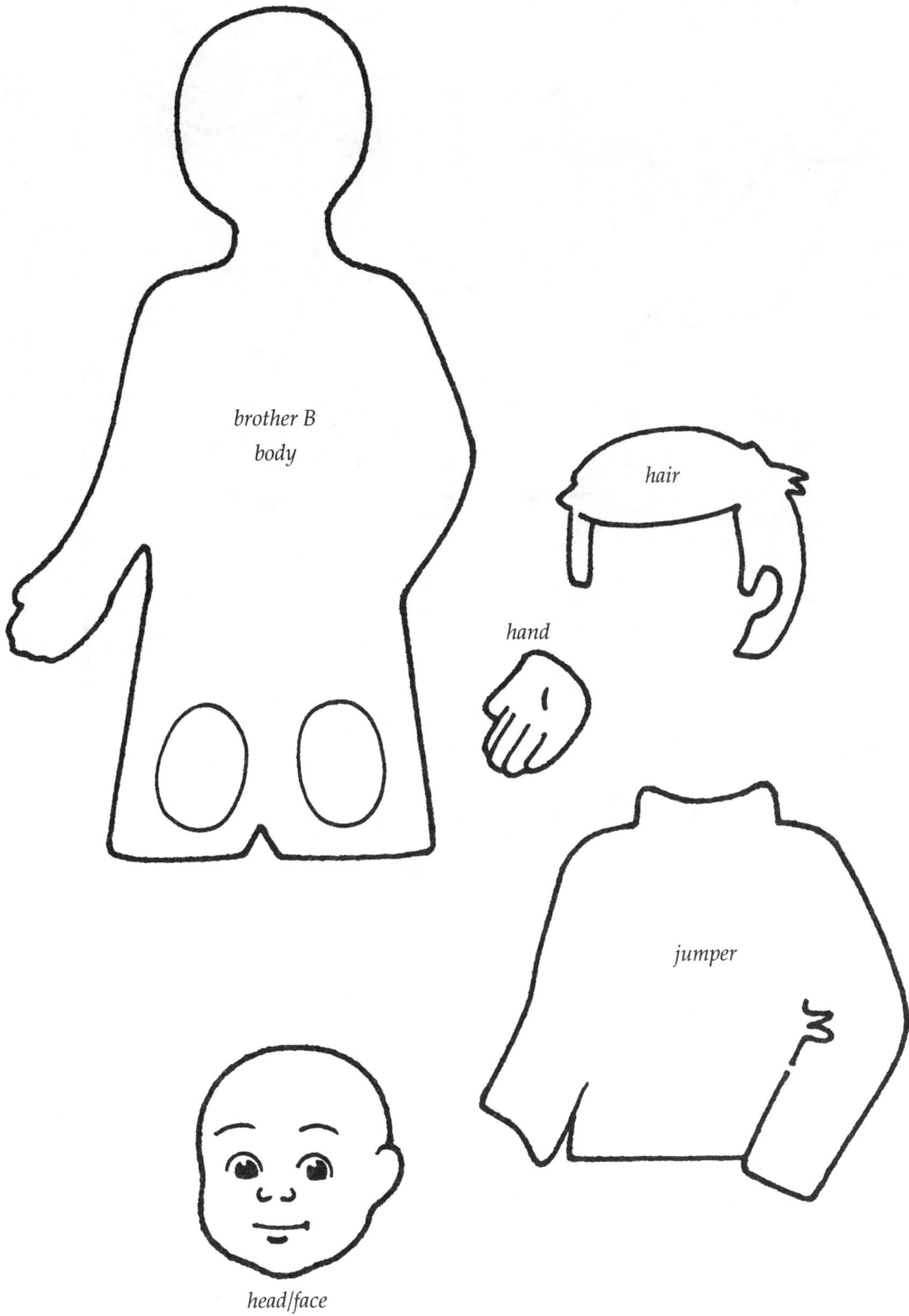

Template – The Two Brothers

Template - The Two Brothers

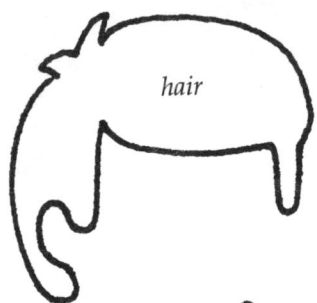

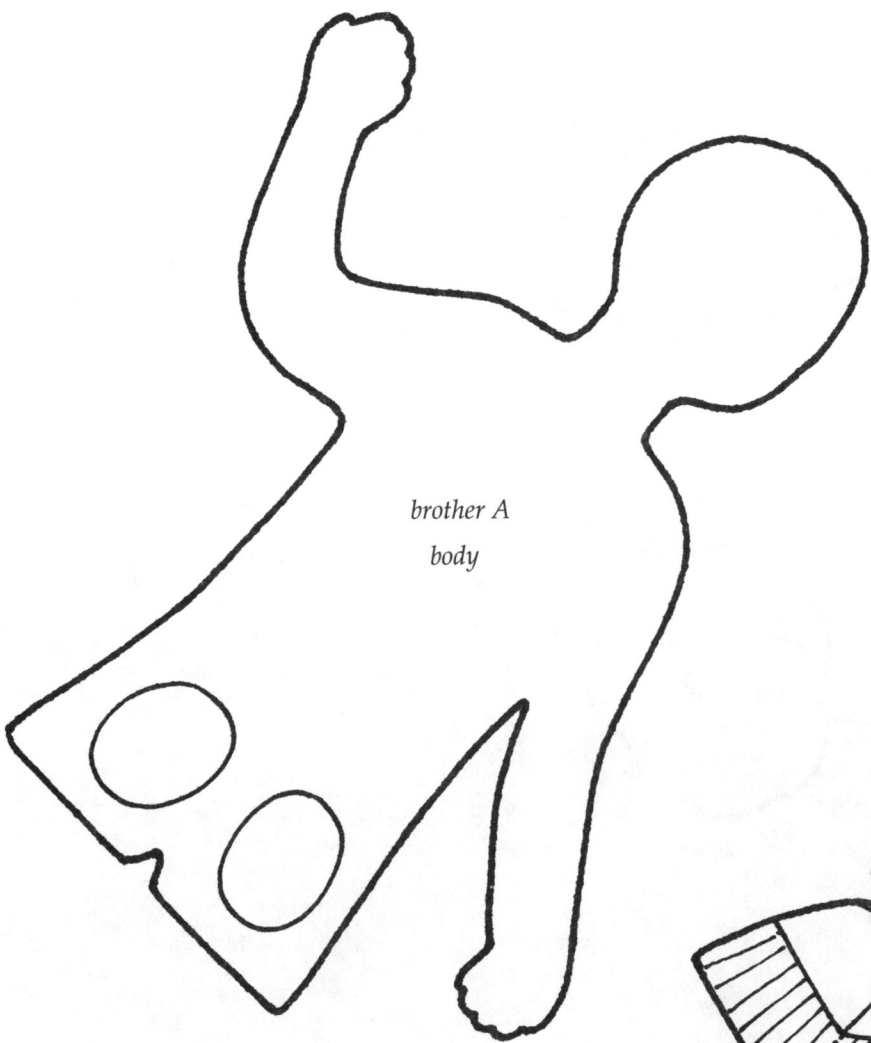

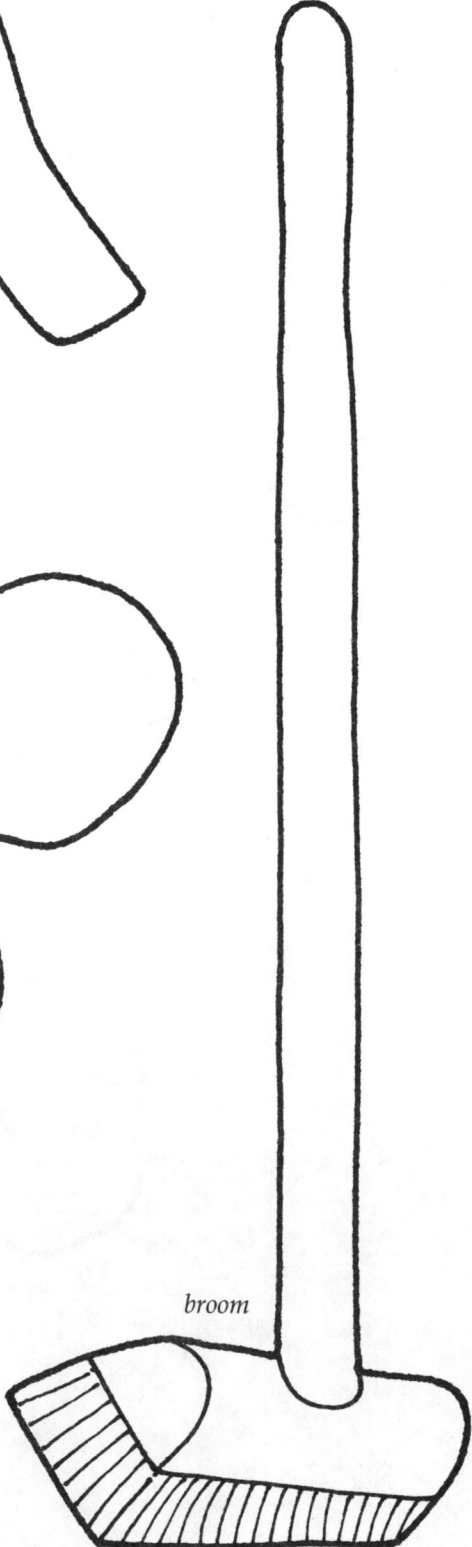

hair

face

jumper

brother A
body

broom

Who is my neighbour?

The Good Samaritan   *Luke 10:25-37*

We have retold this story in a way that is appropriate to under 5s. Look back at the question which provokes Jesus to tell this story in verse 29. Read verses 34-35 to see how personally the Samaritan gets involved. Can you think of any situations when your group could show that they are good neighbours, such as welcoming a new family into the group?

Tell the story

Introduction:
Show various different times on the clock and ask the children and parents what time it is. Ask if any of them were helping anyone at 10 o'clock yesterday or today, such as being friendly to a new child at playgroup. Perhaps at 12 o'clock they were helping to put out the knives and forks for lunch. At 5 o'clock perhaps they were helping by tidying up toys. Today's story is about somebody who helped.

Story:
❶ Tell a story something like this one: Thumper the rabbit was on his way to visit his Uncle Herbert who lived at the bottom of the Great Oak Tree. Thumper was taking his uncle some of his mother's home-made bramble pie. He had to walk through the fields at the back of Mr Thompson's farm. He thought that he heard a rustling in the bushes. His ears pricked up, but he heard nothing more. Suddenly a fox jumped out on to Thumper and he fell over and banged his head on a stone. Luckily the fox was frightened by a tractor in Mr Thompson's field and he ran off, leaving Thumper lying on the ground. But the fox did take the home-made bramble pie. Thumper

Theme
God expects us to love others

Let's sing!
❝ God's love is like a circle ❞
❝ Jesus' hands were kind hands ❞
❝ I'm glad that I live in a house ❞

Activity
Make a helpful dog.

Visual aids
☆ soft toys or puppets: rabbit, fox, horse, sheep, dog
☆ a large clock

Helpful resources
❝ The Good Samaritan: The Wonderful Stories of Jesus ❞ New Testament Book 1
❝ The Lion Book of Stories of Jesus ❞ Chapter 24

couldn't move.
❷ Winston the horse was out for his morning gallop in one of the fields nearby. He enjoyed his daily run. He galloped around and jumped over the fence right in front of Thumper. "Help at last," Thumper thought. Winston looked at the rabbit as he lay there. "Oh dear," he said, "poor thing," and carried on with his daily gallop.
❸ Soon, Thumper heard the baaing of a sheep. It came skipping and jumping by. He stopped to look at him. "Poor

rabbit," he baaed, "it is a shame I can't stop, because I am going to give my coat to be made into a woolly jumper. I have to rush." And off he went.

❹It was getting quite hot, and Thumper was feeling a little faint. He heard another animal coming. It was Tess, the old stray dog. "Oh dear," Thumper thought to himself, "what can I do now?" Dogs didn't usually like rabbits. The dog sniffed at the little rabbit to see if he was still alive. When he saw that he was, he found a picnic container left by some picnickers, and dragged it down to the little brook that ran nearby. He filled it with water and took it back to Thumper so that he could have a drink. The dog licked Thumper's wounds, carefully took him between his teeth and carried him to the farmhouse door. Tess put him down and barked at the door until Mrs Thompson opened it. "Hello, Tess," she said, "what have you there?" Mrs Thompson carried Thumper inside and cleaned him up. She gave him something to eat, and put him in a dry box for the night. Tess watched over him the whole time.

❺Next morning Thumper felt much better and slowly and carefully hopped out of the box. "There you are, Tess," said Mrs Thompson, "the rabbit is feeling much better now. I'll look after him." Tess ran off into the woods, knowing that Thumper was in safe hands.

☞ *Use the puppets or soft toys to act out the story to keep the attention of the children.*

A dog with a wagging tail

Prepare in advance
❶Cut out the dog templates, body, head and tail, in scrap card.
❷Mark on points for head and tail and make holes for pins.

Get the room ready
Put out for each child/parent:
• 1 dog head
• 1 dog tail
• 1 dog body

• 2 brass split pins
Put out on the table:
• crayons
• pencils

What each child/parent does
❶Draw dog face on head.
❷Colour in dog as required.
❸Join head and tail on to body using the split pins.
❹Write name on dog.

You will need
☆ white card: A2 sheet makes 6 dogs
☆ something to make holes in the card
☆ brass split pins, 2 per dog
☆ crayons
☆ pencils

head on top

tail joined behind

head
cut one

tail
cut one

body
cut one

Template – The Good Samaritan

A lady and her pennies

A Lady's Pennies   *Mark 12:41-44*

This is a story about the amount of money that two people give, but not in the way we might expect. Verse 41 tells us where this story takes place. What do verses 43-44 tell us about the difference Jesus sees between the rich man and the widow?

Tell the story

Introduction:
Introduce three friends, Sam, Joel and Jason. Explain how they were all playing happily in the park one day when Sam tripped over, broke his leg, and had to go to hospital. Jason is going to visit Sam in hospital, so he gets his big money box, full of money, and takes out two large coins. "I can spare this, and my bank is still full," he says. So, he goes off and buys a present for Sam in hospital, but he makes sure that everybody knows where he is going... Joel gets his piggy bank and out falls one small coin. This is the last of his birthday money from his granny. "I'll buy Sam a tube of Smarties," he says, and his mum helps him make a card. The boys both go to visit Sam in hospital.

Story:
❶ Continue by saying that Jesus told a story like

Theme
Jesus is happy when we share whatever we have

Let's sing!
❝ Lord, you gave me joy in my heart ❞
❝ 1-2-3 Jesus loves me ❞
❝ Lord, we come to worship you ❞

Activity
Make a lady/boy Smartie money box.

Visual aids
☆ 3 friends: dolls or teddies
☆ 2 piggy banks, one containing a lot of money, one containing only one small coin
☆ a large expensive present and shop-bought "Get-well-soon" card
☆ a tube of Smarties and a home-made card
☆ 2 glove puppets, for the Pharisee and the lady
☆ a collection box and some money

---

this one, only his story was about a rich Pharisee and a poor lady. Tell the story quite simply, in your own words. You will probably want to include these stages:
• many rich people who had plenty to spare were dropping money into the collection
• a poor lady dropped in her last two pennies
• Jesus said that the poor lady put in more than all of the rich men, because they gave what they could spare, but she gave all she had.
❷ Conclude by talking very briefly about the

way that we share things with others. For example, "Today you are going to make a money box out of a tube of Smarties, but before we can save our pennies, you can enjoy eating the Smarties. Will you share yours? Would you give somebody your last Smartie?"

Smartie tube money boxes

Prepare in advance

❶ Cut the light blue sticky paper into rectangles 10cm by 13cm and 3cm by 6cm.

❷ Cut out in scrap cardboard templates for arms, face, hair, trousers, headdress and feet.

❸ Cut out two faces per money box in flesh coloured sticky paper.

❹ Cut out arms in light blue card.

❺ Cut out headdress and trousers in dark blue sticky paper.

❻ Cut out boy's hair in black/brown sticky paper.

❻ Cut out feet in black card.

Get the room ready

Put out for each child/parent:
- 1 Smartie tube
- 1 pair of arms
- 2 faces
- 2 rectangles, 1 each size, of blue sticky paper
- 1 lady's headdress
- 1 pair of trousers
- 1 set of feet

Put out on the table:
- PVA glue and spreaders
- pencils

You will need

☆ a full tube of Smarties per child
☆ light blue sticky paper
☆ light blue card: A4 sheet makes 10 pairs of arms
☆ flesh coloured card: A4 sheet makes 15 sets of faces
☆ dark blue sticky paper
☆ black or brown sticky paper
☆ thick black card: A4 sheet makes 30 pairs of feet
☆ PVA glue and spreaders
☆ pencils

What each child/parent does

❶ Take the large rectangle of blue sticky paper and stick it around the tube, completely covering it.

❷ Stick on arms.

❸ Take the smaller rectangle of blue paper and stick it over the arms.

❹ On the same side stick the trousers.

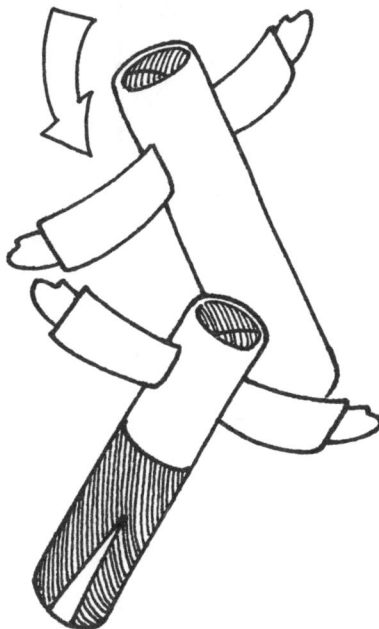

❺ Take the two faces, stick the hair on one and headdress on the other.

❻ Draw face features on to both faces and stick the face on. The boy's face goes on the trouser side.

❼ Put glue around the bottom rim of the tube and stick on the feet. Your box now shows both the lady and the little boy who gave all they had.

☞ *Suggest that the children don't eat their sweets until the end of the session.*

If your church is raising money for something, perhaps a charity or a building project, then you could encourage them to fill the empty tubes with pennies and bring them back to the group to be given away together. This would help to show that the group is a part of the whole church.

Activity Sheet – A Lady's Pennies

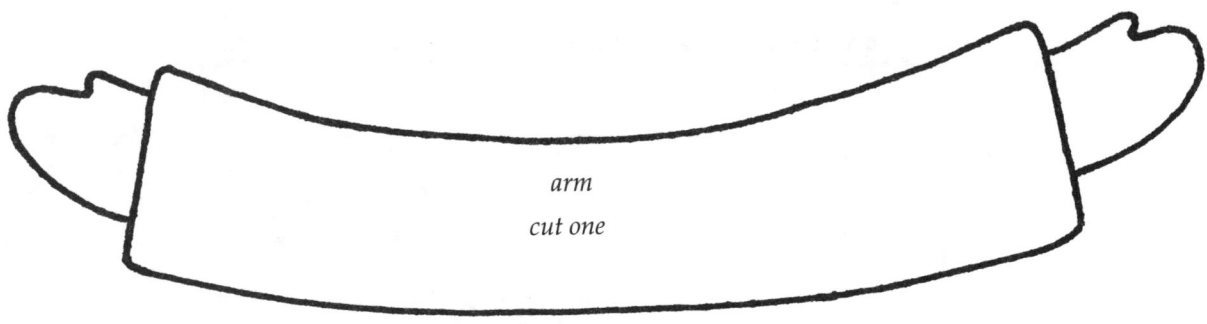

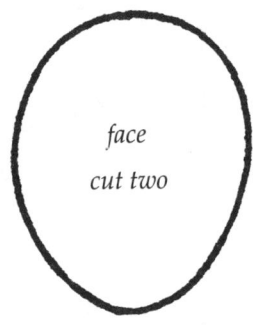

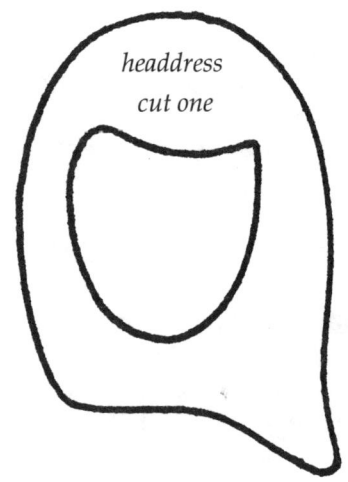

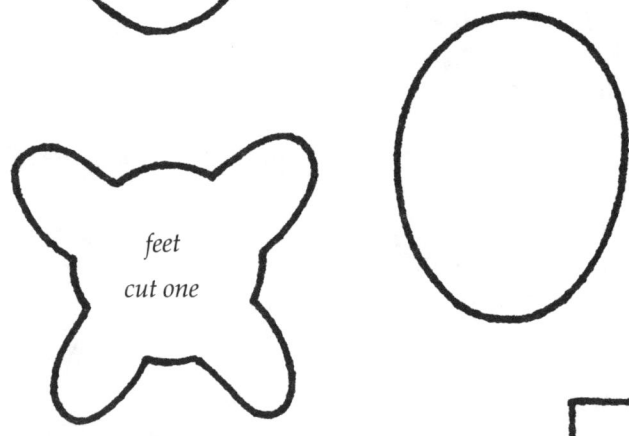

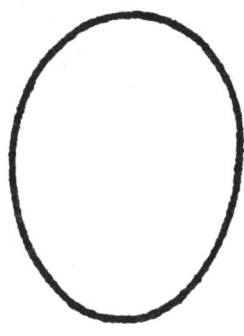

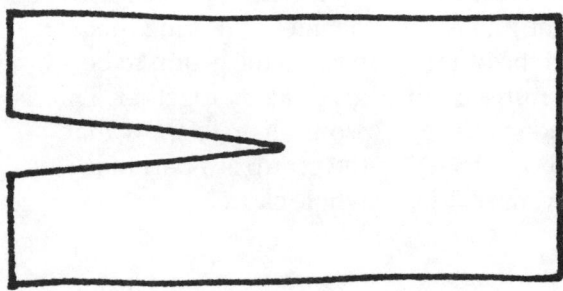

Template – A Lady's Pennies

arm
cut one

face
cut two

hair
cut one

headdress
cut one

feet
cut one

The two builders

The Houses on the Rock and the Sand   *Matthew 7:24-27*

Apart of the town we live in is built on sand, but with modern building techniques this is not too much of a problem. But this story is as appropriate today as it was in Jesus' time. Would you build a house without asking a builder or architect first? Read the story again and notice particularly verses 24 and 26 where Jesus introduces each part of the story. Do you think that the man who built on sand would do it again ?

Tell the Story

Preparation:
Put sand at one end of the bath or sandpit, not packing it down too hard. At the other end put the rocks. Have the two duplo houses half constructed, the wise man's house being on the duplo base. The story itself is very straight-forward, but very visual.

Story:
❶ Two men decide to build houses.
❷ The first man builds his house on a rock, making sure it has a good foundation. (Finish building the wise man's house and put it on the rock.)
❸ The other man builds his house on the sand, but is in such a hurry that he gives it no foundation. (Finish the house very haphazardly, and put it

Theme
Jesus our friend will never let us down

Let's sing!
" The wise man built his house upon the rock "
" I am a lighthouse "
" My God is so big, so strong and so mighty "

Activity
Make hats in the shape of houses and coastline.

Visual aids
☆ a large baby bath or sand pit
☆ a large plastic sheet if you can't do this activity outside
☆ dry sand
☆ rocks
☆ two duplo men
☆ some duplo bricks to build two houses but only one base
☆ child-sized watering cans
☆ buckets holding water
☆ You will need someone other than the story teller to supervize the water

Helpful resource
" The House on the Rock "

on the sand.)
❹ Then the rains come. (Using the water from the watering can, aim at the house on the rock which should stay upright.) The house on the rock is solid. (Water the other house and the surrounding sand. Keep watering until it falls down.) The house on the sand, though, falls down.
❺ The man who built his house on the rock was a wise man, but the man who built on the sand was foolish. This is like the way we build our lives: if we build them on Jesus, he is a firm foundation for us, and he will never let us down.

Sing:
"The wise man built his house upon the rock" with actions.

House hats

Prepare in advance

❶ Cut each A2 sheet of blue card into 3 long strips.

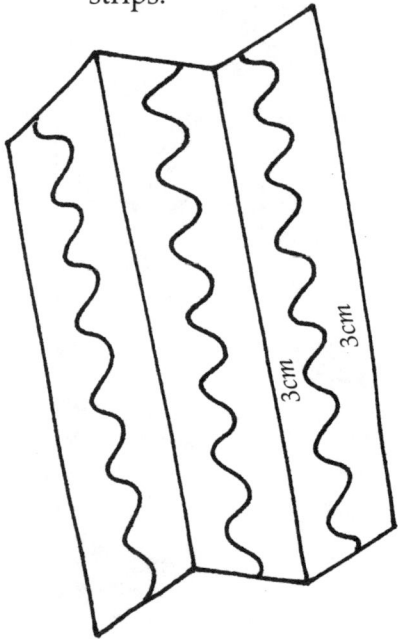

3cm *3cm*

❷ Down the centre of each strip draw a large wave pattern, keeping it at least 4cm away from the edge. Cut along this pattern to make 2 hats.

❸ Cut out the template of the house and then cut out as many houses as you need in yellow card. You will need 2 houses per hat.

❹ Cut out the roof template. Cut out roofs in red sticky paper.

❺ Cut out rectangular doors for the houses, about 3cm by 4cm, in the green or blue sticky paper.

❻ Cut out 4 windows for each house, about 2cm square, in the yellow sticky paper.

❼ Cut the black or brown sticky paper into strips about 3cm by 15cm. You should get 5 per sticky sheet.

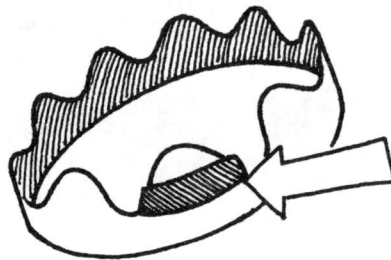

You will need

☆ blue card - an A2 sheet will make 6 hats
☆ yellow card or scraps of yellow, brown, orange, green, to make the house shapes
☆ red sticky paper for the roof
☆ yellow sticky paper for the window
☆ green or blue sticky paper for the door
☆ brown or black sticky paper for the rock
☆ staplers
☆ pencils

Get the room ready

Put out for each child/parent:
• 1 wavy sea hat
• 2 houses
• 2 red roofs
• 2 blue or green doors
• 8 yellow windows
• 1 black or brown strip for the rock

Put out on the table:
• staplers
• pencils

front of hat

back of hat

What each child/parent does

❶ Take a house shape and stick on roof, windows and doors.

❷ Repeat for your second house.

❸ Take the wavy sea hat, and across one of the waves stick the rock. Staple the house on to the rock.

❹ Make up the hat to fit on the child's head. Staple the ends of the hat together.

❺ Take the second house and staple in position at the back - falling down.

❻ Write each child's name inside the hat.

4cm

door
cut two

house

cut two

roof cut 2, red

2cm

2cm

window
cut 8

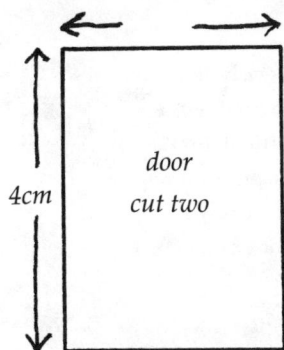

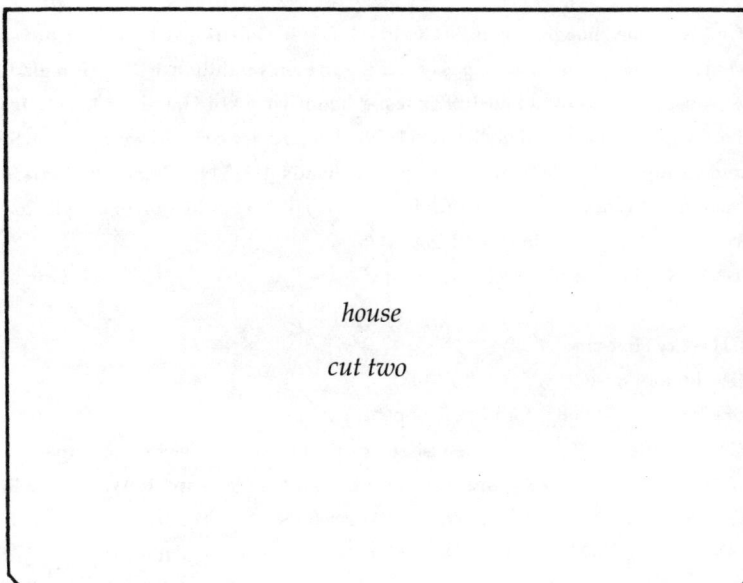

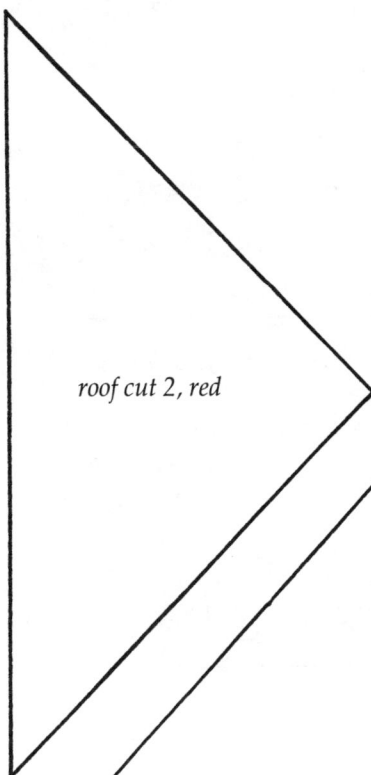

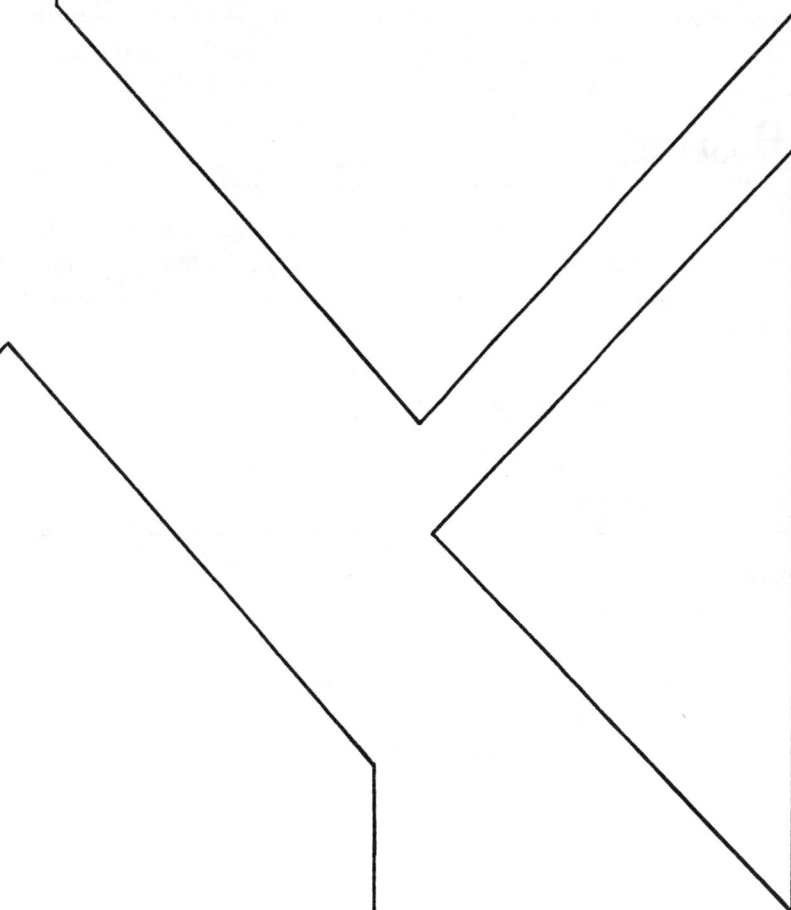

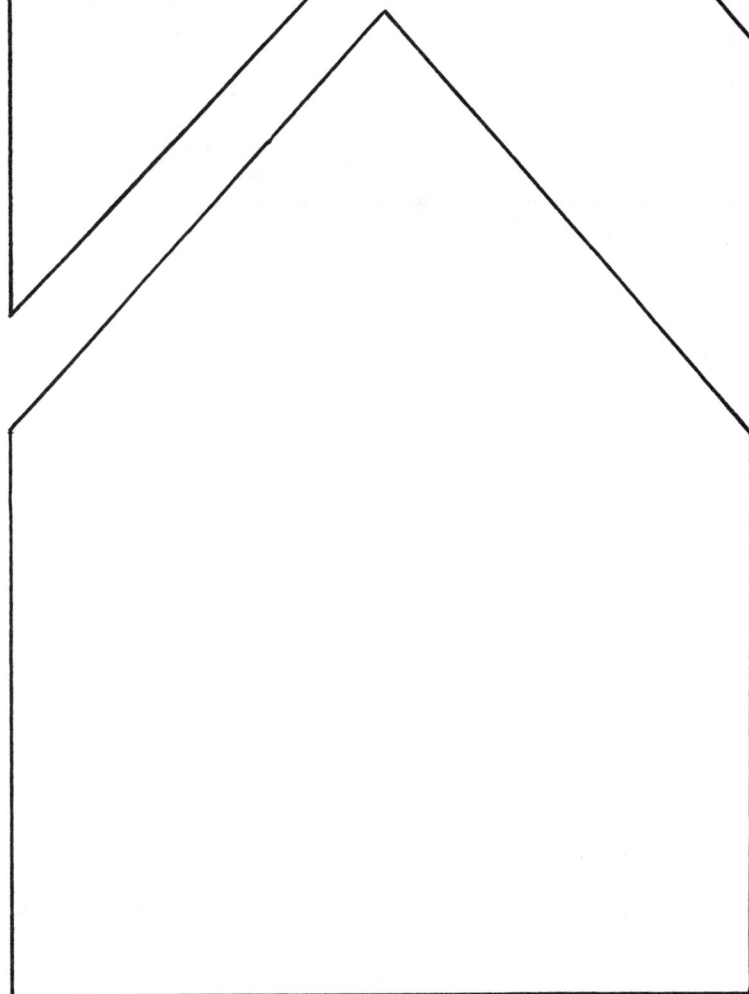

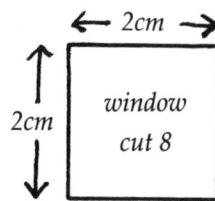

Template – The Two Builders

Bibliography

Songlist

God is for me, though I am little CH 100 (1) (2) (5); **God is good, we sing and shout it** JP 55 (2); **God's love is like a circle** (5); **Have you seen the pussy cat?** JP (5); **I am a lighthouse** JP 87; **I'm glad I live in a house**; **I have hand**s (4); **I was lost but Jesus found me** JP 125; **Jesus' hands were kind hands** JP 134 (4); **Jesus' love is very wonderful** JP 139 (2); **Lord you gave me joy in my heart** SFLT 27 (3); **Lord, we come to worship you** SFLT 28 (3); **My God is so big, so strong and so mighty** JP 169 (2) (5); **Stand up, clap hands** JP 225 (4); **Thank you Lord for this fine day** JP 232 (1); **The wise man built his house upon the rock** JP 252; **Two little eyes to look to God** JP 262; **Who made the twinkling stars?** (4); **Who's the king of the jungle?** JP 289 (2) (5);

1-2-3 Jesus loves me JP 189 (1) (4)

CH = Cry Hosanna

JP = Junior Praise

SFLT - Ishmael's Songs for Little Troopers

(1) = recorded on 'God is for Me' cassette by the Fisherfolk (Celebration Tapes - CT 22032)

(2) = Sing to the King - Richard and Sue Sutton and Linda Grant, 10 Wellington Road, St Albans, AL1 5NI

(3) = Ishmael's Songs for Little Troopers - cassette Songs of Fellowship/Kingsway SFC 212

(4) = Jesus Loves Me - the Keynotes, St John's Harbourne (available through CPAS)

(5) = Praise You, Lord - the Keynotes, St John's Harbourne (available through CPAS)

(6) = Praise Him - cassette Integrity Music Just For Kids IMK 002 (available through Word UK)

Booklist

The House on the Rock, Butterworth and Inkpen, Marshall Pickering; *Where's Spot*? Eric Hill, Picture Puffin 1983; *The Lost Sheep*, Butterworth and Inkpen, Marshall Pickering; *The Palm Tree Bible - The Wonderful Stories of Jesus from the New Testament*, Book 1 (formerly Good News from Jesus), Palm Tree Press 1989; *The Lion Book of Bible Stories and Prayers*, Lion Publishing 1980; *The Two Sons*, Butterworth and Inkpen, Marshall Pickering; *The Lion Book of Stories of Jesus*, Lion Publishing; *Cry Hosanna*, Betty Pulkingham/Mimi Fara, Hodder and Stoughton 1980; *Ishmael's Songs for Little Troopers*, Ishmael, Kingsway Music 1990; *Junior Praise*, Marshall Pickering 1986

Resources and addresses

Glove Puppet Kits, Celebration Arts, P O Box 68, Redhill, Surrey, RH1 4YT

Help I Can't Draw Books 1,2,3, available through CPAS

Under Fives Welcome! Kathleen Crawford, Scripture Union 1990

Under Fives and their Families A CPAS Handbook, Judith Wigley, Marshall Pickering 1990

Telling Stories to Children, Marshall Shelley, Lion Publishing 1990

The Parables of Jesus - Pictures of Revolution, David Wenham, Hodder and Stoughton 1989

Text © 1991 Sue Kirby
This edition © 1991 CPAS

Published by
Church Pastoral Aid Society
Athena Drive
Tachbrook Park
Warwick
CV34 6NG

First edition 1991
ISBN 0-907750-68-0

Illustration reproduced on page 5
from *Alfie's Feet* by Shirley Hughes,
published by The Bodley Head Ltd

Editorial, design, typesetting
and production by
AD Publishing Services Ltd
0296 434553/661273

Cover illustration by
Christine Garlick

Printed by City Print
(Milton Keynes) Ltd